Eva

LIFESIGNS

LIFESIGNS

Intimacy, Fecundity, and Ecstasy in Christian Perspective

Henri J. M. Nouwen

AN IMAGE BOOK
Doubleday
NEW YORK   LONDON   TORONTO   SYDNEY   AUCKLAND

AN IMAGE BOOK

Published by Doubleday, a division of Bantam Doubleday Dell Publishing Group, Inc., 666 Fifth Avenue, New York, New York 10103.

IMAGE, DOUBLEDAY and the portrayal of a cross intersecting a circle are trademarks of Doubleday, a division of Bantam Doubleday Dell Publishing Group, Inc.

Motif drawn by Mona Mark
Book Design by Catherine Hopkins

Library of Congress Cataloging-in-Publication Data

Nouwen, Henri J. M.
    Lifesigns—intimacy, fecundity, and ecstasy in
        Christian perspective.

    1. Spiritual life—Catholic authors.   I. Title.
BX2350.2N673   1986   248.4'82   86-4572

BG

To Madame Pauline Vanier

Acknowledgments

This book has not been written in isolation. Many people have given me much encouragement, support, and assistance. I want to express here my sincere thanks to all of them.

My first word of thanks is to Jean Vanier, who gave me the central themes of this book, introduced me to l'Arche, and encouraged me in my writing. I am deeply grateful for his inspiration, friendship, and generous support.

Most of this text was written during visits to the l'Arche community in the small French village of Trosly-Breuil. I found there not only the necessary time and space, but also the caring and prayerful milieu which is needed to write about the life of the Spirit. A special word of thanks goes to Barbara Swanekamp, who constantly reminded me that "wasting time with God and the poor people of God" is essential for spiritual writing, and to Simone Landrien, who helped me to see in more than one way the mysterious presence of God among the "little ones." Their friendship and personal interest in my work has been a very important source of inspiration for me.

The manuscript of this book has gone through many phases. The efficient and careful secretarial work of Margaret Studier and Gerri Burke Wright enabled the manuscript to move through these phases without interruption, and allowed a series of short reflections to grow into a book. I am grateful to both of them.

As in almost all of my previous publications, Philip Zaeder has been of great help. His numerous literary suggestions give me much to be grateful for. In addition, my editor Robert Heller offered much valuable help during the last phase of this book.

Finally and most emphatically, my thanks go to my friend and co-worker Peter Weiskel, who has done most of the work to prepare this book for publication. While I wrote in Trosly, Peter managed things in Cambridge. He coordinated the typing, did most of the editing, and saw that all details were attended to. Without his competence, patience, and perseverance, this book could not have been completed.

I dedicate this book to Madame Pauline Vanier, Jean Vanier's mother. Her gracious hospitality, her affection for handicapped people and their assistants, her vital interest in world affairs, her strong faith in a loving God, and her very personal friendship and support have showed me most concretely the lifesigns described in this book.

CONTENTS

LIFESIGNS

INTRODUCTION

*From the House of Fear
to the House of Love*

We are fearful people. The more people I come to know and the more I come to know people, the more I am overwhelmed by the negative power of fear. It often seems that fear has invaded every part of our being to such a degree that we no longer know what a life without fear would feel like. There always seems to be something to fear: something within us or around us, something close or far away, something visible or invisible, something in ourselves, in others, or in God. There never seems to be a totally fear-free moment. When we think, talk, act or react, fear always seems to be there: an omnipresent force that we cannot shake off. Often fear has penetrated our inner selves so deeply that it controls, whether we are aware of it or not, most of our choices and decisions.

In many, often very subtle ways fear victimizes and controls us. Fear can make us upset and angry. It can drive us into depression or despair. It can surround us with darkness and make us feel close to destruction and death. Fear can become so intolerable that we are willing to do anything to be relieved from it—even kill ourselves. It not seldom appears as a cruel tyrant who takes possession of us and forces us to live in his house. In fact, most of us people of the twentieth century live in the house of fear most of the time. It has become an obvious dwelling place, an acceptable basis on which to make our decisions and plan our lives.

But why are we so terribly afraid? Why is it so hard to find fearless people? Would there be so much fear if it was not useful to somebody? I have raised these questions ever since I became conscious of the gripping fear in myself and others. Gradually, I began to see the simple fact that those I feared had a great power over me. Those who could make me afraid could also make me do what they wanted me to do. People are afraid for many reasons, but I am convinced that the close connection between power and fear deserves special attention. So much power is wielded by instilling fear in people and keeping them afraid. There are so many fearful children, fearful students, fearful patients, fearful employees, fearful parents, fearful ministers, and fearful believers. Nearly always, a threatening figure stands behind them and holds them under control: a father, a teacher, a doctor, a boss, a bishop, a church or God. Fear is one of the most effective weapons in the hands of those who seek to control us. As long as we are kept in fear we can be made to act, speak, and even think as slaves.

The agenda of our world—the issues and items that fill newspapers and newscasts—is an agenda of fear and power. It is amazing, yes frightening, to see how easily that agenda becomes ours. The things and people we think about, worry about, reflect upon, prepare ourselves for, and spend time and energy on are in large part determined by a world which seduces us into accepting its fearful questions. Look at the many "if" questions we raise: "What am I going to do if I do not find a spouse, a house, a job, a friend, a benefactor? What am I going to do if they fire me, if I get sick, if an accident happens, if I lose my friends, if my marriage does not work out, if a war breaks out? What if tomorrow the weather is bad, the buses are on strike, or an earthquake occurs? What if someone steals my money, breaks into my house, rapes my daughter, or kills me?" Listen also to the many "how" questions: "How can I raise children in a world threatened by total destruction? How can I prevent another conflict, another war, or a nuclear holocaust? How can I keep the Russians from coming too close? How can I succeed on my own as an adult? How can I keep my good name among my neighbors? How can I make it to heaven?"

A huge network of anxious questions surrounds us and begins to guide many, if not most of our daily decisions. Clearly, those who can pose these fearful questions which bind us within have true power over us. For hidden under their questions lies the threat that not following their directions will make our worst fears come true. Once we accept these questions as our own, and are convinced that we must find answers to them, we become more and more settled in the house of fear. When we consider how much our educational, political, religious, and even social lives are geared to finding answers to questions born of fear, it is not hard to understand why a message of love has little chance of being heard.

Fearful questions never lead to love-filled answers; underneath every fearful question many other fearful questions are hidden. Once I have decided that in order to have a child I must be able to offer that child a college education, I get caught in many new, anxious questions involving my job, the place I live, the friends I make, and so on. Once I have come to the conviction that the Russians are the main threat to our national security, many new, fearful questions concerning military, economic, and diplomatic matters emerge. Once I believe that God is out to get me for my bad behavior, complicated moral schemes start to occupy my mind. Once I conclude that I cannot be happy without influential friends, I am in for quite an anxiety-provoking social life. Thus, fear engenders fear. Fear never gives birth to love.

If this is the case, the nature of the questions we raise is as important as the answers to our questions. Which questions guide our lives? Which questions do we make our own? Which questions deserve our undivided attention and full personal commitment? Finding the right questions is as crucial as finding the right answers.

A careful look at the gospels shows that Jesus seldom accepted the questions posed to him. He exposed them as coming from the house of fear. "Who is the greatest in the kingdom of heaven? How often must I forgive my brother if he wrongs me? Is it

against the law for a man to divorce his wife on any pretext whatever? What authority do you have for acting like this? At the resurrection, to which of those seven [men she married] will she be a wife, since she had been married to them all? Are you the king of the Jews? Lord, has the hour come? Are you going to restore the kingdom to Israel? . . ." To none of these questions did Jesus give a direct answer. He gently put them aside as questions emerging from false worries. They were raised out of concern for prestige, influence, power, and control. They did not belong to the house of God. Therefore Jesus always transformed the question by his answer. He made the question new—and only then worthy of his response.

Though we think of ourselves as followers of Jesus, we are often seduced by the fearful questions the world presents to us. Without fully realizing it, we become anxious, nervous, worrying people caught in the questions of survival: our own survival, the survival of our families, friends, and colleagues, the survival of our church, our country, and our world. Once these fearful survival questions become the guiding questions of our lives, we tend to dismiss words spoken from the house of love as unrealistic, romantic, sentimental, pious, or just useless. When love is offered as an alternative to fear we say: "Yes, yes, that sounds beautiful, but . . ." The "but" reveals how much we live in the grip of the world, a world which calls Christians naïve and raises "realistic" questions: "Yes, but what if you grow old and there is nobody to help you? Yes, but what if you lose your job and you have no money to take care of yourself and your family? Yes, but what if refugees come to this country by the millions and disrupt the ways we have been living for so long? Yes, but what if the Cubans and Russians become powerful in Central America and start building their missiles in our own backyard?"

When we raise these "realistic" questions we echo a cynical spirit which says: "Words about peace, forgiveness, reconciliation, and new life are wonderful but the real issues cannot be ignored. They require that we do not allow others to play games with us, that we retaliate when we are offended, that we are always ready for war, and never let anyone take away the good life we have so carefully built up for ourselves." But as soon as these so-called "real issues" begin to dominate our lives, we are back again in the house of fear, even though we keep borrowing words of love, and continue to experience vague desires to live in the house of love.

This book is based upon the conviction that love is stronger than fear, though it may often seem that the opposite is true. "Perfect love casts out all fear" says St. John in his first letter. In this book I hope to search for signs of this perfect love and look for ways to follow those signs. I hope to show the possibility of a spiritual movement: the movement out of the house of fear into the house of love.

But is it possible in the midst of this fear-provoking world to live in the house of love and listen there to the questions raised by the Lord of love? Or are we so accustomed to living in fear that we have become deaf to the voice that says: "Do not be afraid." This reassuring voice, which repeats over and over again: "Do not be afraid, have no fear," is the voice we most need to hear. This voice was heard by Zechariah when Gabriel, the angel of the Lord, appeared to him in the temple and told him that his wife Elizabeth would bear a son; this voice was heard by Mary when the same angel entered her house in Nazareth and announced that she would conceive, bear a child, and name him Jesus; this voice was also heard by the women who came to the tomb and saw that the stone was rolled away. "Do not be afraid, do not be afraid, do not be afraid." The voice uttering these words sounds all through history as the voice of God's messengers, be they angels or saints. It is the voice that announces a whole new way of being, a being in the house of love, the house of the Lord.

Why is there no reason to fear any longer? Jesus himself answers this question succinctly when he approaches his frightened disciples walking on the lake: "It is I. Do not be afraid" (John 6:21). The house of love is the house of Christ, the place where we can think, speak, and act in the way of God—not in the way of a fear-filled world. From this house the voice of love keeps calling out: "Do not be afraid . . . come and follow me . . . see where I live . . . go out and preach the good news . . . the kingdom of God is close at hand . . . there are many rooms in my Father's house. Come . . . take for your heritage the Kingdom prepared for you since the foundation of the world."

The house of love is not simply a place in the afterlife, a place in heaven beyond this world. Jesus offers us this house right in the midst of our anxious world.

What then are the signs by which we come to know the house of love? Are there ways we can gradually overcome our fears and let love be our guide? The following chapters respond to these questions with three words: intimacy, fecundity, and ecstasy. These three words were first given to me by Jean Vanier, the founder of l'Arche (the French word for "the Ark"), a worldwide network of communities for mentally handicapped people.

I had never met Jean Vanier, but we had been in contact through mutual friends. One day Jean called me and said: "I am making a short, Pentecost retreat with some of the l'Arche assistants. Would you like to join us?" He added with a chuckle, "You do not have to say one word!" I flew to Chicago and made the retreat. Though it was our first contact, Jean and I hardly spoke with each other. But in the midst of the silence he gave me the three words around which this book is written. He mentioned them more in passing than to make an important statement. Jean said: "Working with mentally handicapped people, I have come to recognize that all human beings, whatever their condition, are called to intimacy, fecundity, and ecstasy." At first, these concepts seemed little more than good-sounding words that could be easily remembered. But much later, when I read Jesus' farewell address to his disciples, it struck me that Jesus himself describes life in the house of love as a life of intimacy, fecundity, and ecstasy.

Speaking of himself as the vine and of his disciples as the branches, Jesus says: "Make your home in me, as I make mine in you" (John 15:4). This is an invitation to intimacy. Then he adds: "Those who remain in me with me in them, bear fruit in plenty" (John 15:5). This is a call to fecundity. Finally, when he says: "I have told you this so that my own joy may be in you and your joy may be complete" (John 15:11), he promises ecstasy. The more I read and reflected on the Gospel of John, the more I became aware of the importance of these three themes. Once alerted to them by Jean Vanier I recognized them as golden threads woven through the whole of John's gospel.

Since that first short conversation with Jean, much has happened. A true friendship has developed, and l'Arche has become an increasingly important part of my life. After a few visits to the l'Arche community in Trosly-Breuil, France, where Jean lives, I was invited to live there for a year. This stay, which began in August of 1985, has afforded me the time to write this book. Therefore, l'Arche is the main inspiration for these reflections on the spiritual life, and the main source of my stories, examples, and illustrations.

I hope that these chapters on intimacy, fecundity, and ecstasy will begin to show what life in the house of love looks like, and will create the desire to live it.

PART ONE

INTIMACY

Introduction

When Jesus says: "Make your home in me as I make mine in you," he offers us an intimate place that we can truly call "home." Home is that place or space where we do not have to be afraid but can let go of our defenses and be free, free from worries, free from tensions, free from pressures. Home is where we can laugh and cry, embrace and dance, sleep long and dream quietly, eat, read, play, watch the fire, listen to music, and be with a friend. Home is where we can rest and be healed. The word "home" gathers a wide range of feelings and emotions up into one image, the image of a house where it is good to be: the house of love.

But in this world millions of people are homeless. Some are homeless because of their inner anguish, while others are homeless because they have been driven from their own towns and countries. In prisons, mental hospitals, refugee camps, in hidden-away city apartments, in nursing homes and overnight shelters we get a glimpse of the homelessness of the people of our century.

This homelessness, however, is also visible in much less dramatic ways. While teaching university students who came from many different states and countries, I was struck how lonely they were. For many years they live in small rooms, surrounded by strangers, far away from their families and friends. There is little privacy and even less community in their lives. Mostly, they have no contact with children or elderly people. Seldom do they belong to a welcoming neighborhood or a supportive faith community, and only very few know families where they can drop in anytime and feel at home. I have come to consider this situation in which thousands of young adults live as "normal," but when I examine it a little closer it is not hard to understand why so many feel rootless and even lost.

Probably no word better summarizes the suffering of our time than the word "homeless." It reveals one of our deepest and most painful conditions, the condition of not having a sense of belonging, of not having a place where we can feel safe, cared for, protected, and loved.

The first and most obvious quality of a home is its intimacy. When we say: "I do not feel at home here" we express an uneasiness that does not permit intimacy. When we say: "I wish I were home" we express a longing for that intimate place that offers us a sense of belonging. Even though many people suffer much from conflicts at home, even though much emotional suffering finds its roots at home, and even though "broken homes" are increasingly blamed for crimes and illnesses, the word "home" continues to carry with it a warm love and remains one of the most evocative symbols for happiness. The Christian faith even calls us to experience life as "going home" and death as "coming home at last." In Rembrandt's painting of the Prodigal Son, we can see a moving expression of that faith. The loving embrace in which the old father holds his exhausted son affirms our deepest desires for a lasting, intimate home.

To explore in more depth the meaning of intimacy as the first aspect of living in the house of love, I will first show how fear prevents intimacy from developing. Then I would like to have a closer look at the relationship between intimacy and love. Finally I hope to speak about solidarity as the other side of intimacy.

Intimacy and Fear

Fear is the great enemy of intimacy. Fear makes us run away from each other or cling to each other but does not create true intimacy. When Jesus was arrested in the garden of Gethsemane, the disciples were overcome by fear and they all "deserted him and ran away" (Matthew 26:56). And after Jesus was crucified they huddled together in a closed room "for fear of the Jews" (John 20:19). Fear makes us move away from each other to a "safe" distance, or move toward each other to a "safe" closeness, but fear does not create the space where true intimacy can exist. Fear does not create a home. It forces us to live alone or in a protective shelter but does not allow us to build an intimate home. Fear conjures either too much distance or too much closeness. Both prevent intimacy from developing.

My own experience with people whom I fear offers plenty of examples. Often I avoid them: I leave

*the house, move to a corner where I can remain un-
noticed, or express myself in flat, noncommittal sentences. Sometimes I create a false closeness with
them. I talk too long with them, laugh too loudly at
their jokes, or agree too soon with their opinions.
Whether I create too much distance or too much
closeness, I always sense a lack of inner freedom
and a resentment toward the power they have over
me.*

Fearful distance and fearful closeness are even
more noticeable in the larger context of our lives.
Prisons, mental hospitals, and refugee camps are
often built far away from the places where "normal"
people live, to keep the fear-evoking strangers at a
safe distance. Other types of safe distance abound:
safe topics to discuss, safe issues to get involved in,
safe subjects to write about, safe people to invite,
and so on. On the other hand, one can find the safe
closeness of the clique, the sect, or the club, places
where people huddle together in mutual admiration
or common suspicion of the outsider. In a time like
ours, when fear takes on an apocalyptic dimension,
it is extremely tempting to join a small group that
calls non-members useless, dangerous, or evil and
offers a unique sense of belonging to those who follow the rules.

But whether through distance or closeness, fear
prevents us from forming an intimate community in
which we can grow together, everyone in his or her
own way. When fear separates or joins us, we can

no longer confess to each other our sins, our broken-ness, and our wounds. How, then, can we forgive each other and come to reconciliation? Distance allows us to ignore the other as having no significance in our lives, and closeness offers us an excuse for never expressing or confessing our feelings of being hurt.

Jean Vanier, who has lived for more than twenty years with mentally and physically handicapped people, has become a keen observer of this dynamic of fear. He saw that these severely handicapped people seem like strangers living in another world, like prisoners caught behind the bars of their own deformation, like sick people who cannot help themselves, like poor and helpless beggars who make no contribution to society. He saw how they evoke fear in the hearts of those who regard themselves as normal: the "regulars," the free, the healthy, the rich, and the successful. He saw how they remind us of another reality to be avoided at all cost.

Jean Vanier realized that as long as these handicapped men and women remain "the others," they become the victims of cold institutions or of suffocating overprotection. He noticed how they are rejected as aliens or clung to as personal property. He understood that either way no true home exists for them. Their otherness robs them of the free space where they can grow according to their own pace, their own rhythm, and their own, often hidden gifts.

In 1964 Jean Vanier decided to offer a home to two handicapped people, Raphaël and Philippe. It was a decision that took a long time to mature. After ten years in the British and Canadian navies, he had studied philosophy at the Catholic Institute in Paris and had become a professor at St. Michael's College in Toronto. But he was still unclear about his true vocation. One summer he went to Trosly-Breuil, a little French village one hour north of Paris. Under the guidance of his spiritual director Père Thomas Philippe, who lived there as chaplain to a house for handicapped men, he decided to leave his teaching position and invite Raphaël and Philippe, who for many years had lived in a mental institution and had no family or friends, to form a small foyer (home) with him. It was an irreversible decision. He knew he could never send these two men back to where they had come from.

He called his first foyer "l'Arche," thus indicating that he wanted his home to be like Noah's ark, a refuge for fearful people. Jean did not think about starting a movement or a large organization. He simply began caring for two people who could not manage without permanent help. But soon, people arrived from different countries to offer him help and to start new foyers. Now there are many such homes all over the world—in Canada, Australia, the United States, Haiti, the Dominican Republic, Honduras, Mexico, England, Ireland, Belgium, France, Denmark, Spain, Switzerland, Germany, Italy, the Ivory Coast, Burkina Faso, and India. These homes are created to offer an intimate place to people whose handicap is different from ours.

When Jean Vanier speaks about that intimate place, he often stretches out his arm and cups his hand as if it holds a small, wounded bird. He asks: "What will happen if I open my hand fully?" We say: "The bird will try to flutter its wings, and it will fall and die." Then he asks again: "But what will happen if I close my hand?" We say: "The bird will be crushed and die." Then he smiles and says: "An intimate place is like my cupped hand, neither totally open nor totally closed. It is the space where growth can take place."

It is difficult to offer such a place, precisely because we are fearful and find it hard to let the stranger enter our place and reveal to us our own fears. But when we are willing to confess both to ourselves and the other that we too are broken, that we too have a handicap, and that we too need a place to grow, we can build a home together and offer each other an intimate place.

Intimacy and Love

If fear is the great enemy of intimacy, love is its true friend. Yet the words love and intimacy are used so casually in our heavily psychologized milieu that it requires special care to reclaim their spiritual meaning. We might be tempted to place intimate love on the same level as fear and suggest that it occupies the middle ground between "too distant" and "too close." Intimate love would thus avoid the fearful extremes of a cold distance and a suffocating closeness and offer a happy medium.

Many contemporary reflections on interpersonal relationships betray this way of thinking. They seem to say: "We need each other, but we should not lose our independence; we have a need for closeness, but we should not give up our individuality; we have a need for mutual support, but we also need enough space for ourselves." Although this is true,

*the suggestion is that good interpersonal relation-
ships are the result of negotiation between partners,
in which they define each other's rights as well as
needs. Thus the place of intimate love is constantly
threatened by fear, whether it comes from the right
side or from the left.*

But intimacy is not found on the level where fear
resides. Intimacy is not a happy medium. It is a way
of being in which the tension between distance and
closeness is dissolved and a new horizon appears.
Intimacy is beyond fear. Those who have experienced the intimacy to which Jesus invites us know
that they no longer need to worry about getting too
close or becoming too distant. When Jesus says: "Do
not be afraid; it is I," he reveals a new space in
which we can move freely without fear. This intimate space is not a fine line between distance and
closeness, but a wide field of movement in which the
question of whether we are close or distant is no
longer the guiding question.

When St. John says that fear is driven out by perfect love, he points to a love that comes from God, a
divine love. He does not speak about human affection, psychological compatibility, mutual attraction,
or deep interpersonal feelings. All of that has its
value and beauty, but the perfect love about which
St. John speaks embraces and transcends all feelings, emotions, and passions. The perfect love that
drives out all fear is the divine love in which we are
invited to participate. The home, the intimate place,

the place of true belonging, is therefore not a place made by human hands. It is fashioned for us by God, who came to pitch his tent among us, invite us to his place, and prepare a room for us in his own house.

Words for "home" are often used in the Old and New Testaments. The Psalms are filled with a yearning to dwell in the house of God, to take refuge under God's wings, and to find protection in God's holy temple; they praise God's holy place, God's wonderful tent, God's firm refuge. We might even say that "to dwell in God's house" summarizes all the aspirations expressed in these inspired prayers. It is therefore highly significant that St. John describes Jesus as the Word of God pitching his tent among us (John 1:14). He not only tells us that Jesus invites him and his brother Andrew to stay in his home (John 1:38–39), but he also shows how Jesus gradually reveals that he himself is the new temple (John 2:19) and the new refuge (Matthew 11:28). This is most fully expressed in the farewell address, where Jesus reveals himself as the new home: "Make your home in me, as I make mine in you" (John 15:4).

Jesus, in whom the fullness of God dwells, has become our home. By making his home in us he allows us to make our home in him. By entering into the intimacy of our innermost self he offers us the opportunity to enter into his own intimacy with God. By choosing us as *his* preferred dwelling place he invites us to choose him as *our* preferred dwelling place. This is the mystery of the incarnation. It is beautifully expressed during the Eucharist when the priest pours a little water into the wine, saying: "By the mingling of this water and wine may we come to share in the divinity of him who humbled himself to share in our humanity." God's immeasurable love for us is expressed in this holy interchange. God so much desired to fulfill our deepest yearning for a home that God decided to build a home in us. Thus we can remain fully human and still have our home in God. In this new home the distinction between distance and closeness no longer exists. God, who is furthest away, came closest, by taking on our mortal humanity. Thus God overcomes all distinctions between "distant" and "close" and offers us an intimacy in which we can be most ourselves when most like God.

To those who are tortured by inner or outer fear, and who desperately look for the house of love where they can find the intimacy their hearts desire, Jesus says: "You have a home . . . I am your home . . . claim me as your home . . . you will find it to be the intimate place where I have found my home . . . it is right where you are . . . in your innermost being . . . in your heart." The more attentive we are to such words the more we realize that we do not have to go far to find what we are searching for. The tragedy is that we are so possessed by fear that we do not trust our innermost self as an intimate place but anxiously wander around hoping to find it where we are not. We try to find that intimate place in knowledge, competence, notoriety, success, friends, sensations, pleasure, dreams, or artificially induced states of consciousness. Thus we become strangers to ourselves, people who have an address but are never home and hence can never be addressed by the true voice of love.

Here we come to see what discipline in the spiritual life means. It means a gradual process of coming home to where we belong and listening there to the voice which desires our attention. It is the voice of the "first love." St. John writes: "We are to love . . . because God loved us first" (1 John 4:19). It is this first love which offers us the intimate place where we can dwell in safety. The first love says: "You are loved long before other people can love you or you can love others. You are accepted long before you can accept others or receive their acceptance. You are safe long before you can offer or receive safety." Home is the place where that first love dwells and speaks gently to us. It requires discipline to come home and listen, especially when our fears are so noisy that they keep driving us outside of ourselves. But when we grasp the truth that we already have a home, we may at last have the strength to unmask the illusions created by our fears and continue to return again and again and again.

Conversion, then, means coming home, and prayer is seeking our home where the Lord has built a home —in the intimacy of our own hearts. Prayer is the most concrete way to make our home in God.

*This is beautifully described and faithfully prac-
ticed in the hesychastic tradition of the Eastern Or-
thodox Church. The Greek word "hesychia" means
rest, and hesychastic prayer leads us to rest in God.
It is described as a descending with the mind into
the heart, in order to stand there in the presence of
God. Therefore it is also called the prayer of the
heart. The most commonly used words are those of
the Jesus Prayer: "Lord Jesus Christ, have mercy on
me, a sinner," but sometimes shorter sentences are
used, or just the name "Jesus." Centering prayer, as
introduced by Basil Pennington, and the Maranatha
(Come, Lord Jesus) prayer, described by John Main,
are variations of this form of prayer. I mention the
hesychastic tradition here because it offers a unique
discipline to help us seek our home where Jesus has
built his, in our own hearts. Those who have made
the prayer of the heart a daily practice come to experience it as a simple, yet beautiful way to their
true home. It gradually leads us away from the
house of fear and moves us closer to the house of
love, God's house.*

Thus, prayer launches us on an inward journey to
the heart, that intimate home where an unceasing
conversation of love can take place. Prayer leads us
to the knowledge that "all shall be well, and all shall

be well, and all manner of thing shall be well" (Julian of Norwich).

For Jean Vanier and the handicapped people with whom he lives, this divine intimacy where all is well is the basis for a life together. They have learned that it is impossible to live together as wounded people if they simply depend on each other to provide the intimate home they seek. Our wounds, whether visible or hidden, are too deep for us to offer each other a place totally free from fear. We often put superhuman demands on each other and when these demands are not met we feel hurt and rejected. In a community of deeply handicapped people this is especially visible. Handicapped people ask for constant attention and are often unable to express gratitude or return favors. Bonds that last cannot be based simply on good, better, or excellent interpersonal relationships but must be rooted outside the many devices and desires of the wounded human heart. Rooted in a bond that existed before and beyond human togetherness, bonds of true intimacy rest in the divine covenant. This is the covenant of God's faithfulness expressed in the promises made to Noah, Abraham and Sarah, Moses and the prophets, and made fully visible in the incarnation of Jesus.

God alone is free enough from wounds to offer us a fearless space. In and through God we can be faithful to each other: in friendship, marriage, and community. This intimate bond with God, constantly nurtured by prayer, offers us a true home. We can live together in this home without asking for much more than a willingness to constantly confess our weaknesses to each other and to always forgive each other. Jean Vanier considers this divine covenant the basis of every form of human faithfulness. We can only stay together when the "staying power" comes from the One who comes to us to stay. When we know ourselves to be deeply anchored in that divine covenant, we can build homes together. Only then can our limited and broken love reflect the unlimited and unbroken love of God.

Intimacy and Solidarity

When we use the word "intimacy" in our daily lives we easily associate it with privacy, smallness, coziness, and a certain exclusiveness. When someone refers to a conversation or a party as intimate we tend to think about a few people, a small space, or confidential subject matter. The word "intimate" usually suggests the opposite of being open to the public.

But here our spiritual experience shows us something quite new. Those who have entered deeply into their hearts and found the intimate home where they encounter their Lord, come to the mysterious discovery that solidarity is the other side of intimacy. They come to the awareness that the intimacy of God's house excludes no one and includes everyone. They start to see that the home they have found in their innermost being is as wide as the whole of humanity.

Just as distance and closeness are no longer valid distinctions within God's house, so intimacy and solidarity are no longer valid distinctions either. It is of great importance to see the inner connection between intimacy and solidarity. If we fail to recognize this connection our spirituality will become either privatized or narrowly activist and will no longer reflect the full beauty of living in God's house.

The best way to see the interconnectedness of intimacy and solidarity is to recall and enter more deeply into the words of St. John: "The Word was made flesh and pitched his tent among us" (1:14). These words express the mystery that God, in whom all was created, has become part of that same creation. God, who was rejected by our sins, became sin for us in order to offer us a share in the divine life. Thus, in Jesus Christ all humanity has been gathered and led toward God's house. Through the incarnation of God in Jesus Christ all human flesh has been lifted up into God's own intimacy. There is no human being in the past, present, or future, in East, West, North, or South, who has not been embraced by God in and through the flesh of the Word.

The life, death, and resurrection of Jesus manifest to us the full intimacy of this divine embrace. He lived our lives, died our deaths, and lifted all of us up into his glory. There is no human suffering that has not been suffered in the agony of Jesus on the cross, no human joy that has not been celebrated by Jesus in his resurrection to new life. There is no human death that Jesus has not died, no human life that Jesus has not lived. In him through whom all has been created, all has been restored to the glory of God.

The mystery of the incarnation reveals to us the

spiritual dimension of human solidarity. Because all humanity has been taken up into God through the incarnation of the Word, finding the heart of God means finding all the people of God. Therefore, a Christ in whom all people are not gathered together is not the true Christ. We who belong to Christ belong to all of humanity. That is why Jesus prayed for his disciples with the words: "[Father,] consecrate them in the truth; your word is truth. As you sent me into the world, I have sent them into the world, and for their sake I consecrate myself so that they too may be consecrated in truth" (John 17:17–19). We cannot live in intimate communion with Jesus without being sent to our brothers and sisters who belong to that same humanity that Jesus has accepted as his own. Thus intimacy manifests itself as solidarity and solidarity as intimacy.

Christians are called to bear witness to the truth that God has gathered all people into one family. Yet wherever we look we see the devastating fear people have of one another. Fear between races, religions, nations, continents. Fear between rich and poor, North and South, East and West. Wherever this fear rules division breeds, leading to hatred, violence, destruction, and war. Everything we read in the papers, hear on the radio, and see on television about the condition of the world seems to confirm the saying: "homo homini lupus," human beings are wolves to each other. And since our human intelligence is inventing ever more ingenious instruments of destruction, humanity comes closer every day to its own annihilation. Not solidarity but fragmentation is the most visible quality of the way people relate to each other.

We need new eyes to see and new ears to hear the truth of our unity, a unity which cannot be perceived by our broken, sinful, anxious hearts. Only a heart filled with perfect love can perceive the unity of humanity. This requires divine perception. God sees his people as one, as belonging to the same family and living in the same house. God wants to share this divine perception with us. By sending the only beloved son to live and die for us all, God wants to open our eyes so that we can see that we belong together in the embrace of God's perfect love.

Living in the intimacy of God's house, we gradually come to know the mysterious truth that the God who loves us with a perfect love includes all people in that love without diminishing in any way the unique quality of God's love for each individual person.

This is probably one of the hardest things for us to understand. In our competitive world we are so used to thinking in terms of "more" and "less" that we cannot easily see how God can love all human beings with the same unlimited love while at the same time loving each one of them in a totally unique way. Somehow we feel that our election involves

*another's rejection, that our uniqueness involves an-
other's commonness. Somehow, we think we can
only fully enjoy our being loved by God if others are
loved less than we are.*

*But the spiritual life breaks through these distinc-
tions made in the context of rivalry and competition.
The spiritual life allows us to experience that the
same God who lovingly embraces all people has
counted every hair of our heads (see Matthew
10:30), and that the same God who cares for everyone without exception, loves each individual with
an exceptional love.*

*The deeper our prayer becomes the closer we
come to this mystery of God's love. And the closer
we are to this mystery the better we can live it out
in our daily life. It frees us to appreciate other people's talents without feeling diminished by them and
to lift up their uniqueness without feeling less
unique ourselves. It allows us to celebrate the vari-
ous ways of being human as a sign of the universal
love of God.*

When we enter into the household of God, we
come to realize that the fragmentation of humanity
and its agony grow from the false supposition that
all human beings have to fight for their right to be
appreciated and loved. In the house of God's love
we come to see with new eyes and hear with new
ears and thus recognize that all people, whatever
their race, religion, sex, wealth, intelligence, or background, belong to that same house. God's house has

no dividing walls or closed doors. "I am the door," Jesus says. "Anyone who enters through me will be safe" (John 10:9). The more fully we enter into the house of love, the more clearly we see that we are there together with all humanity and that in and through Christ we are brothers and sisters, members of one family.

In the house of God we are consecrated to the truth, that is, part of God's betrothal with God's people. The word betrothal—which includes the word troth (truth)—beautifully expresses the personal quality of truth. We truthfully belong together in God. This is the spiritual basis of solidarity.

Here too we find the ground of all Christian action. As prayer leads us into the house of God and God's people, so action leads us back into the world to work there for reconciliation, unity, and peace. Once we have come to know the truth we want to act truthfully and reveal to the world its true nature. All Christian action—whether it is visiting the sick, feeding the hungry, clothing the naked, or working for a more just and peaceful society—is a manifestation of the human solidarity revealed to us in the house of God. It is not an anxious human effort to create a better world. It is a confident expression of the truth that in Christ, death, evil, and destruction have been overcome. It is not a fearful attempt to restore a broken order. It is a joyful assertion that in Christ all order has already been restored. It is not a nervous effort to bring divided people together, but a celebration of an already established unity. Thus action is not activism. An activist wants to heal, restore, redeem, and re-create, but those acting within the house of God point through their action to the healing, restoring, redeeming, and re-creating presence of God.

Jean Vanier understands this very well. When you see the many small homes for the handicapped, you wonder if Jean and his co-workers could not use their time and energy more efficiently. While the needs of the world clamor for our attention, hundreds of capable, intelligent men and women spend their time, often all of their time, feeding broken people, helping them walk, just being with them, and giving them the small comfort of a loving word, a gentle touch, or an encouraging smile. To anyone trying to succeed in our society, which is oriented toward efficiency and control, these people are wasting their time. What they do is highly inefficient, unsuccessful, and even useless. Jean Vanier, however, believes that in this useless work for the poor the truth of God's perfect love for all people is revealed.

This elevated thought is lived out in surprisingly down-to-earth ways. While at l'Arche I was invited to a birthday party for my friend Brad, who works in La Promesse, one of the French foyers. Although the fourteen handicapped people who live there are

from the area, the assistants who live and work with them day in and day out come from six different countries. Some of them speak French poorly, many have college degrees, and all of them are young people.

Since my friend Brad is an American, his housemates decided to make him a real American meal. We had hamburgers with ketchup and potato chips, Pepsi-Cola, and milk shakes. We ate and drank with paper plates, paper napkins, plastic cups, and plastic straws. Although I had never had a meal like that during my eighteen years in the United States, it was a good way to discover how Americans are perceived from afar.

There were thirty people all together and everyone offered something: a gift, a song, a speech, a drawing, a flower, or a skit. There was a lot of good craziness. Would-be waiters carried the first dish in procession, balancing their paper plates on their heads, candles were put on hamburgers—for lack of a cake—plastic bottles functioned as fake microphones, guitars were strummed à la Elvis Presley, and recorders played with or without a melody. The evening was concluded by candlelight with a spiritual song, a gospel reading, spontaneous prayer of petition, and a hymn to Our Lady of l'Arche that sounded as solemn as the Salve Regina in a Trappist monastery.

Sitting there among all those handicapped and nonhandicapped "nuts," jumping up and down, singing, laughing, clapping hands, and praying, it sud-

denly struck me that the poor had gathered the rich around them from all over the world and revealed to them the true love of God. Thus the distinctions between handicapped and normal, poor and rich, inefficient and efficient were dissolved, and the basic unity of all who live in the house of God was made visible. "Irrelevant" lives had acquired a divine relevance, the relevance of a God who is revealed to us in the weakness of a small child, an itinerant preacher, and a crucified outcast.

The intimacy of the house of love always leads to solidarity with the weak. The closer we come to the heart of the One who loves us with an unconditional love, the closer we come to each other in the solidarity of a redeemed humanity.

Conclusion

This brings us to the conclusion of this chapter on intimacy as the first sign of life in the house of love. We came to see intimacy as a divine gift allowing us to transcend fearful distance as well as fearful closeness, and to experience a love before and beyond all human acceptance or rejection. This divine intimacy is neither possessive nor exclusive but opens our eyes to all people as brothers and sisters and frees our hands to work in solidarity with all of humanity, especially with those who are suffering. We are tempted to view prayer as being with God, in contrast to action, which involves being with people. Hopefully, these reflections on intimacy have shown that prayer and action are *both* expressions of an intimate relationship with God, and through God with all of humanity.

This view of intimacy provides a context for exploring the meaning of fecundity, the second sign of life in the house of love.

PART TWO

FECUNDITY

Introduction

"Those who remain in me, with me in them, bear fruit in plenty" (John 15:5). With these words Jesus speaks about fruitfulness or fecundity. When Jesus himself and all humanity through him have become our true home, we can become truly fecund or fruitful people. The word "fecundity" is not used often in daily conversation, but it is a word worth reclaiming, for it can put us in touch with our deepest human potential to bring forth life. That the word fecundity sounds archaic may indicate that the reality to which this word points is receding to the background of our consciousness in today's technological society.

Still, it is not only our sense of homelessness, but also our doubts concerning our ability to give life that cause us so much suffering. Much pain in the world of today is directly caused by this deep sense of worthlessness. Countless people experience their existence as dull, boring, stagnant, and routine. They lack inner vitality, a deep desire to be alive. For them, every day is just another day, often filled with many things to do but seldom offering profound human satisfaction. This is the experience of living without bearing fruit. But, fortunately, some men and women have a deep sense of their value—precisely because they are in touch with the life-giving quality of their existence. Their joy brings forth joy, and their peace brings forth peace. They make us aware of the holy contagiousness of all that lives.

In this chapter I would like to explore in some detail the role of fecundity in our lives. First, I will discuss the negative relationship between fear and fecundity. Then I hope to describe how fecundity manifests itself in the house of love. Finally, I plan to show the missionary implications of fecundity by connecting it with receptivity.

Fecundity and Fear

Fear not only prevents intimacy; it also thwarts fecundity. When fear dominates our lives, we cannot quietly and patiently protect that holy space where fruit can grow. Two ways in which fear manifests itself are sterility and productivity.

Sterility is one of the most obvious responses to fear. When we feel surrounded by threats, we close ourselves off and no longer reach out to others, with whom fruitful relationships might grow. The more afraid we become, the more we withdraw. As we sense the danger increasing, we withdraw more and more until finally we find ourselves totally out of touch with the "other." Thus we regress into self-created protective patterns and become sterile.

Many people experience themselves as sterile, even when they have children, a job, money, and significant success in life. The experience of sterility is the experience of not being truly alive, and therefore of being unable to give life. We often hear remarks such as: "I am not in charge of this world. Others make the big decisions . . . All I ask is to be left alone . . . I like to mind my own business and look after my own interests. I know that people are suffering, but there's nothing I can do about it . . ." This is the voice of death. It expresses a sense of uselessness and self-doubt that gradually extinguishes the desire to grow.

In the First World, with its high technology and its complex bureaucracy, an increasing number of men and women have lost any sense of being active participants in the making of the future. They often experience themselves as useless appendices to a complex machine, the inner workings of which they do not understand. This is not only true for unemployed youth and retired elderly, but also for many who are quite busy in the factories and offices of our contemporary society. Being bored while being busy is an ominous symptom of this spiritual illness.

In the Third World, the sense of uselessness is no less present, though the reason is very different. There, the distance between the poor and the wealthy is often so great that the poor feel superfluous or even burdensome to those who shape their country's destiny. Many people living in dire misery have become fatalistic. They feel that whatever they do their situation will not change. The powers of the mighty seem so overwhelming to them that better education, housing, and health care hardly seem worth fighting for. Real change seems as impossible to them as finding gold at the end of a rainbow.

Whether in the First or the Third World, fear for unknown powers causes the inner experience of sterility, the experience that causes people to say: "I have nothing to offer." Hope ebbs away without the conviction that we have received a promise that will be fulfilled through our lives, and we gradually lose our ability to give life. For some, this leads to a reluctance to have children: "Why have children if there is no future for them?" For others, children become the only source of security: "When I grow old, who will take care of me if not my own children?" But for all, loss of hope involves a stifling of an inner movement toward the future. Sterility, here, is first and foremost a spiritual woundedness. The Spirit of God is a creative spirit, always expressing itself in new life. When that spirit is extinguished by fear, we cling to what we have and thus stop moving and growing.

Jean Vanier explained to me once how Jesus recognized the sterility of the woman at the well (see John 4:1–42). Jesus met her at noon, when it is very hot and nobody comes to the well to fetch water. She came at that time because she did not dare join the town's women, who came early in the morning not only for water, but also for the latest news. She was an outcast not welcome among her own. When Jesus said to her, "The water that I shall give will turn into an inner spring" (John 4:14), he confronted her with her spiritual sterility and offered her healing. At the end of the story we see how this rejected, fearful woman returns to her town and testifies fearlessly: "Come and see a man who has told me everything I ever did; I wonder if he is the Christ?" (John

4:29–30). She is freed of her fear, she is healed of her sterility, and she has become a fruitful witness of the life-giving Christ.

Fear can lead not only to sterility but also to a flight toward productivity. Here we have to make an important distinction between fruits and products. A call to live a fruitful life does not necessarily imply a call to be productive. A product is something we make. Certain concrete actions lead to a product that we can subsequently claim as our own. When we repeat these actions, the result is the same product, and if we repeat these actions over and over, we are soon considered very productive persons who do not waste their time.

In our world, everything can become a product: not only cars, houses, books, and artifacts, but also influential friends, successful interactions, and important decisions. They all can become part of what we have "made," what gives us a sense of being acceptable in the eyes of others. People are often introduced with emphasis on their productivity. "This is Frank, he wrote some very influential books which you might like to read; this is Mary, who won a Pulitzer Prize; and this is Peter, who knows everything about photography, etc., etc. . . ." In all of this, the suggestion is made that we are what we make. In our contemporary society, with its emphasis on accomplishment and success, we often live as if being productive is the same as being fruitful. Productivity gives us a certain notoriety and helps take away our fear of being useless. But if we want to live as followers of Jesus, we must come to know that products, successes, and results often belong more to the house of fear than to the house of love.

When fear dominates our lives, we worry about our value as persons and become easily preoccupied with products. I even wonder if our deep-seated fear of being sterile does not often motivate us to a frantic productivity.

The emphasis on productivity is increasing constantly. Not only in the business and industrial world, but also in the worlds of sports and academics productivity has become the main concern.

My own experience is limited to universities. One of the saddest aspects of the lives of many students is that they always feel pressured. The irony is that those who have the luxury of spending time reading the great books of our culture and exploring the intricate beauty of creation find themselves always fighting deadlines. Students complain about the number of pages they have to read or write, and anxiously wonder how they will finish their many assignments on time. The word "school," which comes from "schola" (meaning: free time), reminds us that schools were originally meant to interrupt a busy existence and create some space to contemplate the mysteries of life. Today they have become the arena for a hectic race to accomplish as much as

possible, and to acquire in a short period the neces-sary tools to survive the great battle of human life. Books written to be savored slowly are read hastily to fulfill a requirement, paintings made to be seen with a contemplative eye are taken in as part of a necessary art appreciation course, and music com-posed to be enjoyed at leisure is listened to in order to identify a period or style. Thus, colleges and uni-versities meant to be places for quiet learning have become places of fierce competition, in which the rewards go to those who produce the most and the best.

This emphasis on productivity has also deeply af-fected our interpersonal relationships. Relationships between husbands and wives, parents and children, brothers and sisters, teachers and students are often poisoned by an all-pervasive concern for success. Even our most intimate and vulnerable moments can be invaded by the fear of not being able to "deliver."

A whole industry has grown up around human sexuality. Movies, videotapes, books, and maga-zines exploiting the sexual desires of men and women are produced and sold in great quantities. They promote the myth that sexual prowess is the fastest way to happiness. The tragedy is that, in a world with so many lonely people, the sex industry

wants us to believe that true intimacy is identical with "good" sex. And even though most people are able to stay away from the pornographic expression of human sexuality, many find themselves suffering, consciously or unconsciously, from the false emphasis on sexual potency that pervades our hedonistic culture.

I do not want to suggest that productivity is wrong or needs to be despised. On the contrary, productivity and success can greatly enhance our lives. But when our value as human beings depends on what we make with our hands and minds, we become victims of the fear tactics of our world. When productivity is our main way of overcoming self-doubt, we are extremely vulnerable to rejection and criticism and prone to inner anxiety and depression. Productivity can never give the deep sense of belonging we crave. The more we produce, the more we realize that successes and results cannot give us the experience of "at homeness." In fact, our productivity often reveals to us that we are driven by fear. In this sense, sterility and productivity are the same: both can be signs that we doubt our ability to live fruitful lives.

Living with Jean Vanier and his handicapped people, I realize how success-oriented I am. Living with men and women who cannot compete in the worlds of business, industry, sports, or academics, but for whom dressing, walking, speaking, eating, drinking, and playing are the main "accomplishments," is extremely frustrating for me. I may have come to the theoretical insight that being is more important than doing, but when asked to just be with people who can do very little I realize how far I am from the realization of that insight. Thus, the handicapped have become my teachers, telling me in many different ways that productivity is something other than fecundity. Some of us might be productive and others not, but we are all called to bear fruit; fruitfulness is a true quality of love.

Fecundity and Love

Just as intimacy does not find its place halfway between closeness and distance, fecundity is not the happy medium between sterility and productivity. Sterility and productivity are both ways to control our lives and determine their direction. A fearful refusal to give birth to new life and a fearful attempt to create it ourselves are both ways to play God. Thus, we keep an anxious distance from the Lover who invites us to surrender ourselves and be led to unknown and unpredictable places.

Fecundity transcends both sterility and productivity, since it belongs to the order of love and not to the order of fear. The great mystery of fecundity is that it becomes visible where we have given up our attempts to control life and take the risk to let life reveal its own inner movements. Whenever we trust and surrender ourselves to the God of love, fruits will grow. Fruits can only come forth from the ground of intimate love. They are not made, nor are they the result of specific human actions that can be repeated. Neither predictable nor definable, fruits are gifts to be received. It is precisely this quality of gift that distinguishes fruits from products.

Let me describe three aspects of the fruitful life: vulnerability, gratitude, and care. A fruitful life is first of all lived in vulnerability. As long as we remain afraid of each other we arm ourselves and live defensive lives. No fruits can come forth from such lives. They lead to walls, arms, and to the most sophisticated inventions, such as Trident submarines and cruise missiles, but they do not bear fruit. Only when we dare to lay down our protective shields and trust each other enough to confess our shared weakness and need can we live a fruitful life together.

The way of God is the way of weakness. The great news of the Gospel is precisely that God became small and vulnerable, and hence bore fruit among us. The most fruitful life ever lived is the life of Jesus, who did not cling to his divine power but became as we are (see Philippians 2:6–7). Jesus brought us new life in ultimate vulnerability. He came to us as a small child, dependent on the care and protection of others. He lived for us as a poor preacher, without any political, economic, or military power. He died for us nailed on a cross as a useless criminal. It is in this extreme vulnerability that our salvation was won. The fruit of this poor and failing existence is eternal life for all who believe in him.

It is very hard for us to grasp even a little bit of the mystery of God's vulnerability. Yet, when we have eyes to see and ears to hear we can see it in many ways and in many places. We can see it when a child is born, the fruit of the love of two people who came together without defenses and embraced each other in weakness. We can see it in the grateful smiles of poor people and in the warm affection of the handicapped. We can see it every time people ask forgiveness and are reconciled.

Much suffering is caused by the fear of confessing and asking forgiveness. I have seen the most radical changes in the lives of people when they finally found the courage to confess what they felt most ashamed of or most guilty about and discovered that instead of losing a friend they gained one. Distances were bridged, walls came tumbling down, and abysses were filled in. I vividly remember many long and painful conversations with a student who kept stressing how much she hated God. For her, God was a morbid oppressor who made her life miserable by burdening her life with shame and guilt. None of my explanations about God's compassion and love were able to change her mind. But one day, when there was ample time to talk, when we both felt free from pressures and when a relationship of trust had begun to develop between us, she told me the long and torturous story of her life in all its painful detail. As she spoke I could sense that gradually something new was being born in her: the deep

awareness that she was truly loved and did not have to be afraid. Later, she wrote me and said: "That long talk we had was the beginning of a new life for me, a life lived under the gaze of a forgiving and always loving God." It was new life for her precisely because the true face of God had become visible in the mutual vulnerability of two human beings. Not only had this young student discovered God, but she had also found a new friend.

Wherever we see people overcoming their fears and approaching each other in mutual vulnerability, we catch a glimpse of the love in the house of God and taste the fruit of that love.

A second aspect of the fruitful life is gratitude. Our preoccupation with success extinguishes the spirit of gratitude. When our hearts and minds are bent on proving our value to others and competing with our rivals, it is hard to give thanks. In a society that presents independence and self-reliance as ideals, gratitude is more a sign of weakness than of strength. Gratitude presupposes a willingness to recognize our dependence on others and to receive their help and support.

Yet as soon as we shift our attention from products to fruits we become grateful people. Jesus always gave thanks. When he stood before the opened grave of Lazarus, he thanked his father for hearing his prayer (John 11:41). When he gathered his disciples for the Last Supper, he spoke words of thanks over bread and wine. Gratitude belongs to the core of the life of Jesus and his followers.

One of the most moving stories about gratitude is the story about the multiplication of bread as told by the Evangelist John (6:5–15). When Jesus saw the hungry crowds and wondered where to buy some bread for the people to eat, Andrew said: "There is a small boy here with five barley loaves and two fish; but what is that for so many?" Andrew's word powerfully summarizes our attitude as fearful people. The needs are enormous, the reserves very small, so what can we do? The implication of this attitude is clearly: let us hold on to the little we have so that we at least survive. But "Jesus took the loaves, gave thanks, and gave them out to all who were sitting ready; he then did the same with the fish, giving out as much as was wanted." This radical shift of vision, from looking at the loaves and fishes as scarce products which need to be hoarded, to seeing them as precious gifts from God which ask to be gratefully shared, is the movement from wreaking death to bringing forth life, the movement from fear to love. When the story ends, with the glorious statement that "the disciples filled twelve hampers with scraps left over from the meal of five barley loaves," there is no doubt left that God's house is a house of abundance, not scarcity.

Gratitude flows from the recognition that all that is, is a divine gift born out of love and freely given to us so that we may offer thanks and share it with others.

The more we touch the intimate love of God which creates, sustains, and guides us, the more we recognize the multitude of fruits that come forth from that love. They are fruits of the Spirit, such as: joy, peace, kindness, goodness, and gentleness. When we encounter any of these fruits, we always experience them as gifts.

When, for instance, we enjoy a good atmosphere in the family, a peaceful mood among friends, or a spirit of cooperation and mutual support in the community, we intuitively know that we did not produce it. It cannot be made, imitated, or exported. To people who are jealous, and who would like to have our joy and peace, we cannot give a formula to produce it or a method to acquire it. It is always perceived as a gift, to which the only appropriate response is gratitude.

Every time we experience real goodness or gentleness we know it is a gift. If we say: "Well, she gets paid to be nice to us," or "He only says such friendly things because he wants something from us," we can no longer receive that goodness as a gift. We grow from receiving and giving gifts.

Life loses its dynamism and exuberance when everything that happens to us is viewed as a predictable result of predictable actions. It degenerates into commerce, a continuous buying and selling of goods, whether physical, emotional, or spiritual goods. Without a spirit of gratitude, life flattens out and becomes dull and boring. But when we continue to be surprised by new manifestations of life and continue to praise and thank God and our neighbor, routine and boredom cannot take hold. Then all of life becomes a reason for saying thanks. Thus, fecundity and gratitude can never be separated.

Finally, fruits need care. To live a fruitful life, we need an environment that keeps us from being afraid and allows the weak, vulnerable fruits within us to grow in strength. Care does not mean manipulation or control. A seed will never grow if we pull it out of the ground daily to check its progress; likewise, the fruits of our own and others' lives will never mature if we want to control every stage of their development. Products need constant maintenance in order to prevent breakdown. Fruits, on the other hand, ask only for the rich soil, water, air, and sunlight of a caring environment in order to flourish. Jesus cared deeply for the people he met. He did not control or dominate them, but through his words and actions offered them an opportunity to search for new directions and make new choices.

When we are no longer dominated by fear and have experienced the first love of God, we no longer need to know from moment to moment what is going to happen. We can trust that good things will happen if we remain rooted in that love. All true education, formation, and healing are ways to let the fruits of love grow and develop to full maturity. All ministry is a caring attentiveness to vulnerable lives, and a grateful receiving of the variety of fruits by which they manifest their beauty.

Here at l'Arche I can see better than ever the beauty of fecundity. When we live in the house of fear, it is hard to imagine how handicapped people without an able mind, an able body, a productive job, or a happy family can be considered fruitful. But those who have lived with handicapped men and women for a long time have come to experience their great fecundity.

I see here how much they give to those who are able to receive. They give generously and without hesitation. They give their hearts. What for us "normal" people often remains hidden behind rationalizations, preoccupations, and fears is for handicapped people the most available gift. They share their love, joy, and gratitude—and also their anxiety, sadness, and disappointment—with such directness that we are challenged to respond from our own hearts. They put us in touch with our often hidden gifts and weaknesses, and become our healers, without even knowing it!

Severely handicapped people often sense the mood of their assistants and the atmosphere in their foyer with an uncanny accuracy. When there is harmony and peace in the house they are happy and

content, but when there is conflict and tension in the air they often pick it up and act it out before their assistants are fully aware of it. They are true barometers of the human spirit. And, as one assistant said: "It is not always easy to live with people who so directly reveal to you your own ups and downs."

Many who have worked for years with handicapped people will gladly say that they have received more than they have given. Sometimes they will even confess that they have found their true selves by working with the handicapped. Jean Vanier told me a story that symbolizes this beautifully. A few years ago, members of l'Arche made a pilgrimage to the Holy Land. When they arrived at the heavily guarded airport in Israel, Jean-Claude, one of the handicapped men, walked right up to the armed Israeli soldiers and started to give each one a handshake, telling them how glad he was to have arrived in the Holy Land! Indeed, very broken people often allow us to see our true selves hidden behind our uniforms and rifles. They tell us that we are really brothers and sisters, and that arms and weapons do not tell the truth of who we are.

Handicapped people are very vulnerable. They cannot hide their weaknesses and are therefore easy victims of maltreatment and ridicule. But this same vulnerability also allows them to bear ample fruit in the lives of those who receive them. They are grateful people. They know they are dependent on others and show this dependence every moment; but their smiles, embraces, and kisses are offered as spontaneous expressions of thanks. They know that all is pure gift to be thankful for. They are people who need care. When they are locked up in custodial institutions and treated as nobodies, they withdraw and cannot bear fruit. They become overwhelmed by fears and close themselves to others. But when they are given a safe space, with truly caring people whom they can trust, they soon become generous givers who are willing to offer their whole hearts.

Handicapped people help us see the great mystery of fecundity. They pull us out of our competitive, production-oriented lives and remind us that we too are handicapped persons in need of love and care. They tell us in many ways that we too do not need to be afraid of our handicap, that we too can bear fruit as Jesus did when he offered his broken body to his Father.

Fecundity and Mission

To come to the full picture of fecundity, we now have to discuss its global dimensions. The fruits of the Spirit of God—joy, peace, patience, kindness, goodness, trustfulness, gentleness, and self-control (Galatians 5:23)—cannot be limited to interpersonal relationships. They have dimensions which far exceed the small circles of friends, family, and community. They carry in themselves a worldwide dynamic that we call mission. As surely as solidarity arises out of true intimacy, mission emerges from fecundity.

One of the most compelling qualities of life in the Spirit of Jesus is that we are always being sent out to bring and receive the gifts of God to and from all peoples and nations. It is spiritually impossible to enter into the house of God and to meet there all of humanity without coming to the inner awareness that the fruits of the Spirit grow and mature in a worldwide process of giving and receiving.

My visits to Latin America have opened my eyes to this global aspect of fecundity. When I first went south, I was fighting feelings of sterility and had a need to prove myself by productivity. I felt that because we in the north have such wealth we are called to share this with the poor of Latin America. I saw lack of material resources, education, and medical care, and responded first with a strong desire to do something about it all. But I discovered quickly that this mindset is like that of the problem solver with all of the "know-how." There is obviously nothing wrong with alleviating poverty and working for better health and education. Yet when our main motivation is to bring about successful changes, we may in the long run do more harm than good, because the urge to bring about change often carries violence in its wake.

If our primary focus is on the fruits of the Spirit, however, we will quickly come to see that they can be found as little and as much among the people of Latin America as among the people of the north. We might even say that in societies where people are so visibly dependent and vulnerable, God's fruitful love often reveals itself with greater ease. After a few weeks among the poor in Lima, Peru, I was so impressed by their gifts of joy, peace, and gentleness—notwithstanding their great needs—that I came to realize that my vocation was as much that of receiver as of giver. Perhaps it was more important for me to receive from the poor the many gifts born of their love than to try to make myself valuable in their eyes.

For us, however, it is far from easy to be receiving people. We so need to take on useful projects,

change inefficient ways, and solve burning problems, that a deep change of heart and mind is re-
quired of us to become receivers. Somehow it seems
hard for us to truly believe that God loves the people
of Central and South America as much as he loves
us, and that his love is as fruitful there as anywhere
else.

When we come to a clear understanding that we
are all brothers and sisters in the house of God—
whatever our race, religion, or nationality—we realize that in God there is no distinction between haves
and have-nots. We all have gifts to offer and a need
to receive. I am increasingly convinced that one of
the greatest misssionary tasks is to receive the fruits
of the lives of the poor, the oppressed, and the suffering as gifts offered for the salvation of the rich.

*It is a tragedy of history that we have proved
more eager to steal the material fruits of the labor of
the poor than to receive the spiritual fruits of their
lives. The degrading term "banana republic" serves
to remind us of this fact.*

We who live in the illusion of control and self-
sufficiency must learn true joy, peace, forgiveness,
and love from our poor brothers and sisters. Martin
Luther King, Jr., considered it just as important for
the blacks in the United States to convert the whites

as to gain equal rights. Likewise, it is as important for the rich to be converted by the poor as it is to share their wealth with the poor. As long as we only want to give and resist becoming receivers, we betray our desire to stay in control at all costs. Thus we remain in the house of fear.

Once I celebrated the Eucharist in memory of an eighteen-year-old man, Antonio, who had been killed in a tragic accident. After the service I walked to the entrance of the church to express my deep-felt sorrow to Antonio's mother. But I was so preoccupied with finding the right words for my own feelings that I kept my eyes on the floor and hardly dared to look at the mother and those who were with her. Finally I stuttered in my poor Spanish: "I really feel deeply about the great loss you have suffered. I have no good words for you, but I hope that you understand that I feel your pain."

My words came out hesitantly and fearfully. The mother, however, interrupted me by saying, "Thank you, Father, thank you very much for the beautiful Mass . . . Would you please come to our house and have dinner with us?" I didn't really hear her words and repeated, "I do feel deeply about the loss of your son." But she said again: "Thank you, thank you for the Mass and come to our home to eat with us." When I still didn't hear her and kept my eyes downcast, she came closer, made me stand straight, looked me in the eyes, and said in a gentle tone: "Don't be so depressed, Father. Don't you know that God loves our Antonio, that God gave him to us for a few years and now wants to bring him to heaven? We are grateful that he was with us and we are grateful too that he can now be with God forever. We are grateful to you also. God loves us all and cares for us all. Please come and have a meal with us."

As I listened I saw her parents, brothers, sisters, her other sons and daughters, and her many grand-children standing around her and looking at me with wide-open, smiling eyes saying: "Yes, Father, yes. She is right. Come and be our guest." Then I realized that this suffering woman, surrounded by those who loved her, was giving me the fruit of her suffering: trust in God, gratitude, gentleness, and care. She was sent to me as much as I was sent to her. She was ministering to me as much as I was ministering to her. She was offering me a word of consolation and strength that only she could speak, since she had suffered so much.

I realized that this woman stood there in the name of countless men and women of Latin America. She was asking us people of the north, who have so much, know so much, and can do so much, to re-ceive the fruits of their struggle and pain and to bring them home with us, so that we too may grow.

How different would our world be if our main concern were to receive the fruits of the love of the poor and oppressed. We are constantly tempted to view poor countries as fertile soil for atheistic communism and threats to our national security. We remain in the house of fear, producing armies, tanks, submarines, and missiles. And the more we produce these products, the harder it becomes to recognize the fruits that ask to be received.

What if we could see our southern neighbors first of all as people who pray with great devotion, who love their children and families deeply, who write lovely poems, and who have a spirit of joy and gratitude? Wouldn't we want to receive these gifts, we who have become too busy to pray, too lonely to keep our families together, too pragmatic for poetry, and too preoccupied with ourselves to be joyful or grateful?

If giving and receiving the fruits of God's intimate love for all people were our main concern, peace would be near. Little of this peace is visible in our world, but wherever and whenever people leave the house of fear and start to share their gifts in the house of love, true mission occurs and true peacemaking begins.

Conclusion

Fecundity brings forth life. God is a God of the living, and wherever God's loving presence becomes known, we see life bursting forth. Both sterility and productivity carry the seeds of death within them. Fecundity always means new life, life that manifests itself in new, fresh, and unique ways: a child, a poem, a song, a kind word, a gentle embrace, a caring hand, or a new communion among the nations.

But life needs to be celebrated. Without celebration, no life can flourish. This brings us to the third quality of life in the house of love: ecstasy.

PART THREE

ECSTASY

Introduction

The third characteristic of life in the house of love is ecstasy. At first this might come as a surprise. When we think of ecstasy we are inclined to visualize mystics in a state of spiritual rapture. We obviously view such states as exceptional and limited to the happy—or unhappy!—few. But I consider it very important to reclaim the word "ecstasy" for all Christian people who strive to move from the house of fear to the house of love. After speaking about intimacy and fecundity, Jesus said to his disciples, "I have told you this, so that my joy may be in you and your joy may be complete" (John 15:11). "Complete joy" is the reward of intimate and fruitful life in the house of God. Ecstasy is this complete joy, a joy not reserved for a few mystics but offered to all believers.

We live in a joyless time. If homelessness and doubts about our ability to give life are two of the main causes of suffering in our world, joylessness has become one of the main signs of that suffering. Moreover, the joy which people *do* experience is seldom described.

I vividly remember how one of my university teachers spoke for a whole year about anxiety in human life. He discussed in great detail the thoughts of Kierkegaard, Sartre, Heidegger, and Camus and gave an impressive exposé of the anatomy of fear. One day, during the last month of the course, a few students found the courage to interrupt him and ask him to speak a little about joy before the course was over. At first he was taken aback, but then he promised to give it a try. The next class he started hesitantly to speak about joy. His words sounded less convincing and penetrating than when he spoke about anxiety and fear. Finally, after two more meetings, he told us that he had run out of ideas about joy and would continue his interrupted train of thought. This event made a deep impression on me, especially since I had such great admiration for my teacher. I kept asking myself why he was unable to teach about joy as eloquently as he had taught about anxiety.

Somehow joy is much harder to express than sadness. It seems that we have more words for sickness than for health, more for abnormal conditions than for normal conditions. When my leg hurts, my head aches, my eyes burn, or my heart stings, I talk about it, often in elaborate ways, but when I am perfectly healthy I have little, if anything, to say about those parts of my body.

Does this mean there is less joy in life than sadness? Perhaps. But it is also possible that joy is in fact a deeper, more intimate, more "normal" condition than sadness and pain, and therefore harder to articulate. Words about joy often sound trite, superficial, or sentimental and seldom seem to touch us as deeply as words about anguish, fear, and pain. They seldom seem to reach the source.

For Jesus, joy is clearly a deeper and more truthful state of life than sorrow. He promises joy as the sign of new life: "You will be sorrowful, but your sorrow will turn to joy. A woman in childbirth suffers, because her time has come; but when she has given birth to the child she forgets the suffering in her joy that a human being has been born into the world. So it is with you: you are sad now, but I shall see you again, and your hearts will be full of joy, and that joy no one shall take from you" (John 16:20b–22).

Jesus connects joy with the promise of seeing him again. In this sense, it is similar to the joy we experience when a dear friend returns after a long absence. But Jesus makes it clear that joy is more than that. It is "his own joy," flowing from the love he shares with his heavenly Father and leading to completion. "Remain in my love . . . so that my own joy may be in you and your joy may be complete" (John 15:9b, and 11).

The word "ecstasy" helps us to understand more fully the joy that Jesus offers. The literal meaning of the word can help to guide our thinking about joy. "Ecstasy" comes from the Greek "ekstasis," which in turn is derived from "ek," meaning out, and "stasis," a state of standstill. To be ecstatic literally means to be outside of a static place. Thus, those who live ecstatic lives are always moving away from rigidly fixed situations and exploring new, unmapped dimensions of reality. Here we see the essence of joy. Joy is always new. Whereas there can be old pain, old grief, and old sorrow, there can be no old joy. Old joy is not joy! Joy is always connected with movement, renewal, rebirth, change—in short, with life.

Joy is essentially ecstatic since it moves out of the place of death, which is rigid and fixed, and into the place of life which is new and surprising. "God is God not of the dead but of the living" (Matthew 22:32). There is no tinge of death in God. God is pure life. Therefore living in the house of God is living in a state of constant ecstasy, in which we always experience the joy of being alive.

In this chapter I would like to explore in some detail the meaning of ecstasy in our lives. First, I would like to show how fear and ecstasy cannot exist together. Then I hope to describe how ecstasy becomes celebration in the house of love. Finally, I would like to discuss the global dimension of ecstasy by viewing it as the way to a new international order.

Ecstasy and Fear

Just as fear inhibits intimacy and fecundity, so too does it make ecstasy impossible. When we say: "We were ecstatic when we saw those mountains" we recall a fearless moment, a moment in which we were totally receptive to the beauty surrounding us. The ecstatic moment is precisely the moment when we lose our self-preoccupation and are drawn out of ourselves into a new reality.

The house of fear has no room for ecstasy. Fear keeps us clinging to the familiar place, or, in the case of acute anxiety, makes us dissipate ourselves aimlessly. In our fear-ridden times, these two reactions —routine and rootlessness—are quite visible.

Routine induces a sense of sameness and familiarity by which fears can be temporarily alleviated. We often use routine ways of talking, ways of thinking, and ways of acting to avoid fearful interactions. Routines are predictable and repeatable and hold no surprises. Remarks such as: "This is the way we do things here," or "It has always been this way," or "I am used to this method," or "I have always learned that . . ." can all point to somewhat static and therefore deadening routines. Sometimes routines take the form of elaborate rituals. Before going to sleep, small children often want their parents to go through certain rituals in order to give them a sense of safety. A story, a prayer, a cookie, a kiss, or a song can all become part of a bedtime ritual to dispel the "spirits" of darkness. Often a child can be adamant about keeping things the same and in the right order.

Yet children are not the only ones who develop such routines. We all do to some degree. Our rituals can be as simple as the way we start a day, offer hospitality, conduct a conversation, or prepare and eat a meal. They can be as complex as the way we think about politics, relate to the church, celebrate feast days, speak about death, or respond to a crisis in our life.

It would be simplistic to view all of these routines as expressions of fear. Many of them are helpful ways of ordering our lives and communicating with others. But when routine behavior begins to dominate our daily lives, and suggestions of change call forth violent resistance, fear has begun to poison the roots of our existence.

At l'Arche, it is easy to notice the way routines are used to deal with fear. Once I was deeply impressed by a thirty-year-old, mentally handicapped man who told me in precise detail the way he performed his task in the workshop. But when I showed my enthusiasm to one of the assistants, she said:

"He always tells that story to newcomers in the house. It is his way of dealing with strangers. We are trying to help him gradually overcome his fear and compose a few more stories to tell." When I heard this I realized suddenly how much this handicapped person was like me. I may have more than one story to allay my fears, but those who know me well often say: "Not that story again!" It seems that I too have my little "success stories" that I use to relieve my anxiety and establish a certain level of acceptance.

The stronger the fear, the more rigid the routines become. When our milieu causes us great anxiety we often cling to familiar ways of thinking and acting.

Once I read a story about two men who decided to cross the Atlantic in a rowboat. In the middle of their journey they lost their sense of direction and were overcome by fear. The only way to prevent themselves from going mad in the midst of the boundless ocean was to create a "mental playpen," a very rigid daily program. They did not leave a minute unplanned. They even decided the subjects of their conversation and the methods of their dialogue. One hour was set aside to exchange personal histories, another to talk about art, another to discuss science. Thus they prevented themselves from losing their mental boundaries and were able to

stay sane until a passing ship spotted them and took them on board.

It is no wonder that many people are strongly attracted to communities in which life is highly structured and ideas are clear-cut. Their deep-seated fears make them quite willing to sacrifice freedom for security.

Jesus encountered this routine behavior in the form of legalism. His conflicts concerning the observance of the sabbath are good examples. When on a sabbath he cured the man born blind, the Pharisees exclaimed, "This man cannot be from God. He does not keep the sabbath" (John 9:16). And when he healed a crippled woman, also on a sabbath, the synagogue official said to the people, "There are six days when work is to be done. Come and be healed on one of those days and not on the sabbath" (Luke 13:14).

While Jesus showed a high regard for the observance of the Jewish law, he attacked fear-and-power-motivated legalism and clearly demonstrated that the law should always be in the service of the divine work of love.

It is easy for us to condemn the Pharisees and even thank God that we are not like them! Yet the psychologist Erwin Goodenough suggests that we

are all legalists most of the time. All of us enjoy the feeling of peace and security that can come from obeying a clear, specific code of conduct, and every society and religious community does its best to provide them. Goodenough compares legalism to a vividly patterned curtain which both shields us from the unknown and shows us how to behave. Jesus, in his view, was a "supralegalist," one who "bursts through the socially provided curtain, at least on some points, to fresh perceptions and judgements." (See Erwin R. Goodenough, The Psychology of Religious Experiences, *New York: Basic Books, 1965, pp. 102–3.)*

Routines have a certain place in our lives. They also offer us a certain safety and comfort, but when they become our main coping device, they make us rigid, even dead. Without any form of ecstasy, we cannot survive very long.

Fear, however, not only leads us to routinized behavior. It can also bring us to its complete opposite: rootlessness. Fear can make us into wanderers who go from one place to another without direction or goal. Our emotions and feelings then become like a wild river that leaves its bed and destroys the land instead of irrigating it. Lashing out, self-mutilation, erratic talking, running away, aimless wandering— all can be responses to a fear that has become too great for us to face.

When Jesus describes the fearful signs preceding

the coming of the Son of God, he warns his disciples not to run here and there in a panicky, rootless way, with hearts coarsened by debauchery, drunkenness, and the cares of life. He urges them to wait in unceasing prayer for the strength to survive all that is going to happen, and to "stand confidently" before the Son of Man (see Luke 21:34–36).

In La Forestière, one of the l'Arche homes in France where deeply handicapped people live, I see how anguish sometimes finds expression in self-mutilation. The assistants have to work hard to protect the men and women, most of whom cannot speak, walk, eat, or dress themselves, from harming themselves. Edith, for instance, regularly beats her head against hard objects. I seldom see her without bandages to cover her self-inflicted wounds and protect her from doing herself more harm.

It is hard to fathom what goes on in the hearts of such persons who have very limited ways of communicating; but just being with them leads me to suspect an existential fear, intense beyond our most compassionate understanding. The anxiety of these broken people gives us a glimpse of Jesus' agony in the garden of Gethsemane. Their anxiety suggests an immense loneliness which nobody can penetrate, a homelessness that goes far beyond the need for a caring friend or a hospitable house, a rootlessness that opens up into chasms of human despair. The most one can do is to be present, not expecting any changes, but standing in loving awe at the immensity of human fear that Jesus came to carry with us to the cross and beyond.

And still, there is joy and peace even at La Forestière. In some mysterious way the handicapped and their assistants form a community of love, stronger than the agonies of its people. It is an expression of the divine presence in which both happiness and sadness are embraced as well as transcended. It has something to do with the cross, which has become for them a sign of hope. Somehow roots exist after all—roots beyond all rootlessness.

Rootlessness cannot lead to joy any more than routine behavior. Without a place to move from and refer to as the home from which we come, every movement can easily become a panicked flight leading nowhere. Rootlessness and goal-lessness are closely connected. People who have lost touch with their roots also tend to lose their sense of direction. This is quite understandable, since our roots offer us a time, place, and context in which to search for new possibilities. It is hard to search for your own way of being at home in the world when you have little or no memory of ever having felt at home. Many young men and women who have lost their motivation to develop their minds and hearts have little sense of home. When the world is a fearful place where you need all of your emotional energy just to survive, you have little capacity to move from one way of being alive to another.

After having lived some months in Peru I was struck by the joylessness of many of my North American friends. Though they had no lack of food, clothes, shelter, or medical care, and although they had more education than most Peruvians will ever have, these young people walked around as if the whole burden of the world was laid on their shoulders. They all looked very seriously preoccupied with many problems, and seemingly responsible for all the major issues that plague our world. Their words were heavy, their reflections somber, their emotions melancholic, their outlook on life pessimistic, and their self-esteem very low. Few felt at home in their own world. Often they suffered from strained relationships with their family, had difficulty in developing close relationships with their peers, and felt hostile toward people in authority. Often they did not feel at home in their own bodies either. In many ways they were estranged, strangers to their past, their present, and their future: no home to come from, no home to go to, no true movement, no true life, no true joy. Seeing and feeling this deep suffering in my ambitious, successful friends, I was increasingly overwhelmed by the immense spiritual crisis of the so-called First World.

Ecstasy and Love

Ecstatic joy is not a happy medium between routine and rootlessness. Joy breaks into our lives from a divine source, and cannot be found in the house of fear where routine and rootlessness dwell. To be sure, many attempts are made to produce joy: happy hours, receptions, and surprise parties are very common in our society. But are not such "productions" attempts to create an atmosphere in which we can forget the past and ignore the future for a few hours, while changing nothing in our basically sad existence? Much money and energy is spent trying to make people happy and relaxed by offering a moment of artificial bliss. This happiness is as contrived as the good meal given to a man on death row before his execution. It tastes good but does not keep him alive.

Many people hardly believe anymore in the possibility of a truly joy-filled life. They have more or less accepted life as a prison and are grateful for every occasion that creates the illusion of the opposite: a cruise, a suspense novel, a sexual experience, or a few hours in a heightened state of consciousness.

This is happiness in the house of fear, a happiness which is "made in the world" and thus is neither lasting nor deeply satisfying.

In our secularized Western society, Christmas offers a good occasion to experience this illusory happiness that offers a short break in our fear-filled lives. For many, Christmas is no longer the day to celebrate the mystery of the birth of God among us, the God hidden in the wounds of humanity. It is no longer the day of the child, awaited with prayer and repentance, contemplated with watchful attentiveness, and remembered in liturgical solemnity, joyful song, and peaceful family meals. Instead, Christmas has become a time when companies send elaborate gifts to their clients to thank them for their business, when post offices work overtime to process an overload of greeting cards, when immense amounts of money are spent on food and drink, and socializing becomes a full-time activity. There are trees, decorated streets, sweet tunes in the supermarkets, and children saying to their parents: "I want this and I want that." The shallow happiness of busy people often fills the place meant to experience the deep, lasting joy of Emmanuel, God-with-us.

The joy that Jesus offers his disciples is his own joy, which flows from his intimate communion with the One who sent him. It is a joy that does not separate happy days from sad days, successful moments from moments of failure, experiences of honor from experiences of dishonor, passion from resurrection. This joy is a divine gift that does not leave us during times of illness, poverty, oppression, or persecution. It is present even when the world laughs or tortures, robs or maims, fights or kills. It is truly ecstatic, always moving us away from the house of fear into the house of love, and always proclaiming that death no longer has the final say, though its noise remains loud and its devastation visible. The joy of Jesus lifts up life to be celebrated.

Celebration is indeed the word we need here. The divine, ecstatic joy of the house of love becomes manifest in celebration. Celebration marks the life of the disciple of Jesus as well as the life of his new community. The disciple leaves behind the old life in search of a new life. The community is *ec-clesia,* a people "called out" from the land of oppression to the land of freedom. For every disciple as well as for the entire fellowship, following the Lord involves celebration, the ongoing, unceasing lifting up of God's love that has proved itself victorious. Celebration is the concrete way in which God's ecstatic joy becomes visible among us.

It is of great importance to reclaim the word "celebration" as one of the core words of the Christian life. Celebration is not a party on special occasions, but an ongoing awareness that every moment is special and asks to be lifted up and recognized as a blessing from on high. There is Christmas, Easter, Pentecost, and the many feast days of the saints. There are countless birthdays, anniversaries, and memorial days. And then there are days to welcome and to say farewell, to receive guests and to visit friends, to start a project and to finish it, to sow and to reap, to open a season and to close it.

But even these moments do not exhaust the full meaning of celebration. Celebration lifts up not only the happy moments, but the sad moments as well. Since ecstatic joy embraces *all* of life, it does not shy away from the painful moments of failure, departure, and death. In the house of love even death is celebrated, not because death is desirable or attractive but because in the face of death life can be proclaimed as victorious.

Here at l'Arche among handicapped people I see much pain, loneliness, anger, frustration, deep anguish, and heart-rending powerlessness. It is all too visible to remain hidden behind the screen of politeness and good behavior. The pain must be faced openly and directly. But it is precisely in this unadorned context that the power of celebration is revealed. At l'Arche it seems as if people are saying: "Yes, life is hard, very hard, day in, day out, with much pain, disappointment, and sadness; but there is never a day that should not be lifted up in gratitude to the giver of life. There is never an hour in which the light is not revealed in the darkness, never a death that cannot bear fruit."

Every night, when the people of a l'Arche household come together around a candle and an icon of Jesus or Mary, songs are sung, the scriptures are read, and prayers are said. Often much sadness is gathered up in these moments: the sadness of Maurice who did not get the visit he had hoped for, the sadness of Marie whose mother is still ill, the sadness of Pierre who refuses to leave his room. Gladness too is expressed: for the good food, for the new assistant, for the new painting, for the friendly visitor, for the lovely gifts, for the fresh flowers. Thus, these night prayers of thanksgiving, petition, and praise reach far beyond the distinction between gladness and sadness to the unspeakable joy that the world can neither give nor take away.

There are always flowers on the table, and often candles or napkins with special names. At first I thought of them as ways of breaking the dull routine of the weeks and months. But I soon realized that here, where people are so obviously broken and in need of healing, no day is lived without a glimpse of new hope, without the sound of a voice that speaks of love, or without the sense that somewhere among us there is a place that can be fully trusted. Whether Brad has his birthday or St. Francis his feast day, whether Alain is leaving or Émile is coming back, whether Advent is starting or Lent is ending, whether Sylvia lost her mother or Gérard had a new baby sister; yes, whether the Lord dies on the Cross or rises from the dead—all must be lifted up and celebrated in an unceasing song of joy, the joy of a life that no illness or death can destroy.

Celebration is not just a way to make people feel good for a while; it is the way in which faith in the God of life is lived out, through both laughter and tears. Thus celebration goes beyond ritual, custom, and tradition. It is the unceasing affirmation that underneath all the ups and downs of life there flows a solid current of joy. The handicapped men and women of l'Arche are becoming my teachers in the most important course of all: living in the house of God. Their joy leads me beyond the fearful place of death, and opens my eyes to the ecstatic potential of all life. Joy offers the solid ground from which new life can always burst. Joy can be caught neither in one feeling or emotion nor in one ritual or custom but is always more than we expect, always surprising, and therefore always a sign that we are in the presence of the Lord of life.

We might be tempted to dismiss this as wishful thinking or blissful dreaming, but those who have tasted the joy I speak about know how real it is, and those who have met truly joyful people also have no doubt about its reality.

Joyful persons do not necessarily make jokes, laugh, or even smile. They are not people with an optimistic outlook on life who always relativize the seriousness of a moment or an event. No, joyful persons see with open eyes the hard reality of human

*existence and at the same time are not imprisoned
by it. They have no illusion about the evil powers
that roam around, "looking for someone to devour"
(1 Peter 5:8), but they also know that death has no
final power. They suffer with those who suffer, yet
they do not hold on to suffering; they point beyond it
to an everlasting peace. Few people have embodied
joy as well as the Dutch Jewish woman Etty Hillesum, who lived in Amsterdam under the Nazi oc-
cupation and in Auschwitz in 1942. In the midst of
the agonies of the pogroms in Holland she writes:*

*"I believe that I know and share the many sor-
rows and sad circumstances that a human being can
experience, but I do not cling to them, I do not pro-
long such moments of agony. They pass through me,
like life itself, as a broad, eternal stream, they become part of that stream, and life continues. And as
a result all my strength is preserved, does not become tagged on to futile sorrow or rebelliousness"
(From* An Interrupted Life: The Diaries of Etty Hillesum, 1941–43, *New York: Pantheon, 1984, p. 81).*

However, joy is not just a quality radiating from
individual persons. It is as much, if not more so, a
gift to the community of believers. "Where two or
three meet in my name, I shall be there with them"
(Matthew 18:20). These words reveal that the ecstatic joy of the house of love is Christ's own joy-
filled presence, made manifest each time we enter
into communion with each other in and through
Christ.

During the last ten years I have come to see how the Eucharist can create deep, lasting community among people.

For many years I thought that the Eucharist was first of all a celebrative expression of an already existing community. Although this is true, my recent experience has shown me that the Eucharist creates community as well as expresses it.

I started a daily Eucharist at two universities with one or two students. Gradually more came, people who did not know each other, and had very different ideas or viewpoints in religious matters, and were quite different in age, nationality, and life-style. Most of these people would never have chosen each other as friends or companions. But they all, often for quite different reasons, felt attracted to a daily Eucharistic celebration, in which the Word of God was proclaimed and the Body and Blood of Christ shared. Over the months these quite different people found themselves drawn by Word and Sacrament into a deep community. They discovered a bond based not on physical or emotional attractiveness, social compatibility or common interests, but on the presence of the living Christ among them. Confessing their sins together, accepting together God's mercy, listening to the Holy Scriptures together, and eating and drinking together from the same bread and cup had molded them into a new community of love.

All of them started to experience support from each other in their daily struggles, many became good friends, and some even found their partners for life. Such were the remarkable fruits of spiritual community. I saw a concrete fulfillment of Jesus' promise: "When I am lifted up from the earth, I will draw all people to myself" (John 12:32).

Community is the place where God completes our lives with his joy. Every word Jesus spoke was spoken to share his own joy with us and thus make our joy complete (see John 15:11). This complete joy is always "ours," that is, it belongs to a life together. Ecstasy is always a movement toward a shared life. Static living separates us and turns us into isolated individuals fighting for our own individual survival. But ecstatic living leads us to the place where new life is discovered "among" us. It makes us break through our walls of isolation and become a people of God, people who proclaim the joy of the eternal life that has already begun. It is the first sign of the kingdom that Jesus came to proclaim.

Still, there is more to say about ecstasy. Ecstasy, like intimacy and fecundity, has a global dimension. It is this global aspect of the ecstatic life that I now want to explore.

Ecstasy and a New International Order

During the same years that I came to know Jean Vanier and his communities for handicapped people, I also became increasingly aware of the global dimensions of human suffering. I witnessed the dehumanizing poverty in Bolivia and Peru, the agonizing struggle of Nicaragua to maintain its hard-won independence, and the genocidal violence in Guatemala. Thus I was confronted with the demonic forces which not only poison relationships between individuals but those between nations as well.

I soon realized that if the word ecstasy is helpful to only individual people and small communities it cannot be the basis of a truly contemporary spirituality. An ecstatic life which ignores the "powers and principalities" eroding creative international relations becomes an escapist life. Though the forces of evil infecting whole nations and peoples are often hidden, complex, and elusive, we are called, as Christians, to unmask and expel them in the Name of the God of love. That is the reason why we must continually search for a Christian spirituality which is global in its dimensions and unafraid to take seriously the dark forces at work on the international level.

It is not hard to see the forces of evil at work. While impressive high-rise office buildings spring up in New York, Chicago, Paris, London, and Amsterdam, more and more people have no house to live in, nor even a mattress to sleep on. While tons of food are dumped to keep prices high, millions die from hunger every year. While billions of dollars are spent to build complex weapon systems for national defense, few resources are devoted to the needs of the homeless, the refugees, the illiterate, the hungry, the elderly, the unborn, the handicapped, the chronically ill, prisoners, and countless people suffering under emotional stress. As the gap between the powerless and the powerful, the poor and the wealthy, the sick and the healthy grows wider, it becomes harder for us to see each other as brothers and sisters, children of a loving God who invites all of us to live in the house of love.

In Guatemala I learned of large cell blocks in the capital city where people torture people day and night with the most sophisticated methods available. Thousands of Guatemalan Indians are being tortured and killed in a systematic attempt to silence the voices crying out for justice and peace.

This does not happen simply because of the criminal inclinations of some power-hungry individuals.

The torturers are also victims of a network of evil that stretches far beyond their understanding.

Recently I heard the story of a young Guatemalan Indian who had been taken away from his family and "made" into a soldier in the Guatemalan Army. He was stripped of all his human dignity by being forced to torture and kill his fellow Indians, under threat of having to suffer the same fate for refusing. Terror made him into a torturer and killer.

When he finally was allowed to visit his family again, his father refused to let him enter his own house. He said: "You can greet your mother, but then you have to leave because you carry death with you." This Indian peasant was rejected by his own people. For them, he had become possessed by the demon of death.

When Satan shows to Jesus all "the kingdoms of the world and their splendor" and says to him: "I will give you all these, if you fall at my feet and worship me" (Matthew 4:9), Jesus never denies Satan's power over the world. And the Apostle Paul does not hesitate to say that our struggle is not "against human enemies . . . but against the Sovereignties and Powers who originate the darkness in this world, the spiritual army of evil in the heavens" (Ephesians 6:12). It is the demonic power of death which holds the world in its claws. It is the "prince of this world" (John 12:31) who is at work.

Here the global dimension of ecstasy emerges. Ecstatic living entails a constant willingness to leave the safe, secure, familiar place and to reach out to others, even when that involves risking one's own security. On an international scale this means a foreign policy that goes far beyond the question "How can our nation survive?" It would be a policy primarily concerned with the survival of humanity and willing to make national sacrifices. It would be a policy which realizes that idolizing the security of the nation endangers the whole of humanity. It would be a policy which places being human before being American, Russian, Cuban, Nicaraguan, or Mexican. In short, it would be a policy that seeks to liberate nations from their mutual fear and offers ways to celebrate our common humanity.

Ecstasy always reaches out to new freedom. As long as national security is our primary concern and national survival more important than preserving life on this planet, we continue to live in the house of fear. Ultimately, we must choose between security—individual, social, or national—and freedom.

Freedom is the true human goal. Life is only true if it is free. An obsessive concern for security freezes us; it leads us to rigidity, fixation, and eventually death. The more preoccupied we are with security the more visible the force of death becomes, whether in the form of a pistol beside our bed, a rifle in our house, or a Trident submarine in our port.

I wrote the following parable to illustrate the disastrous results of an obsessive preoccupation with national security:

Once there was a people who surveyed the resources of the world and said to each other: "How can we be sure that we will have enough in hard times? We want to survive whatever happens. Let us start collecting food, materials, and knowledge so that we are safe and secure when a crisis occurs." So they started hoarding, so much and so eagerly that other peoples protested and said: "You have much more than you need, while we don't have enough to survive. Give us part of your wealth!" But the fearful hoarders said: "No, no, we need to keep this in case of an emergency, in case things go bad for us too, in case our lives are threatened." But the others said: "We are dying now, please give us food and materials and knowledge to survive. We can't wait . . . we need it now!" Then the fearful hoarders became even more fearful, since they became afraid that the poor and hungry would attack them. So they said to one another: "Let us build walls around our wealth so that no stranger can take it from us." They started erecting walls so high that they could not even see anymore whether there were enemies outside the walls or not! As their fear increased they told each other: "Our enemies have

become so numerous that they may be able to tear down our walls. Our walls are not strong enough to keep them away. We need to put bombs on top of the walls so that nobody will dare to even come close to us." But instead of feeling safe and secure behind their armed walls they found themselves trapped in the prison they had built with their own fear. They even became afraid of their own bombs, wondering if they might harm themselves more than their enemy. And gradually they realized their fear of death had brought them closer to it.

While the instruments of death escalate in number, complexity, and scope, enabling us to destroy the human race within a few days, we continue to be preoccupied with defending national boundaries, national pride, and national honor. We forget that the ways we have chosen to defend ourselves endanger us as much as our enemies. Never have nations spent so much to protect themselves against their neighbors near and far, and never have we come so close to the annihilation of the human race.

There is an urgent need for a spirituality that addresses these idolatries and opens the way to a new ecstasy. We must find a way to go beyond our national security obsession and reach out and foster life for all people, whatever their nationality, race, or religion.

We therefore must develop a global spirituality in which the demands of the gospel guide not only the behavior of individuals but of nations as well. Many will consider this naïve. They are glad to accept the teachings of Jesus for their personal and family lives, but when it comes to international affairs they consider these same teachings unrealistic and utopian. Yet, Jesus sent out his apostles to make disciples not just of individual people but of all the nations, and to teach these nations to observe his commands (Matthew 28:19–20). At the last day, Jesus will call these same nations before his throne and raise the critical question: "What have you done for the least of mine?" (Matthew 25:31–46). The life of discipleship goes far beyond individual piety or communal loyalty. The whole world is to be converted! Nations, not just individual people, are called to leave the house of fear—where suspicion, hatred, and war rule—and enter the house of love, where reconciliation, healing, and peace can reign.

The great spiritual leaders, from St. Benedict to St. Catherine of Siena to Martin Luther King, Jr., to Thomas Merton, have all grasped this truth: the power of the renewing Word of God cannot be kept within the safe boundaries of the personal or interpersonal. They call for a new Jerusalem, a new earth, a new global community.

The movement from the house of fear to the house of love has become necessary for the survival of humanity. If we continue to use our many fears—our fear of the Russians, our fear of communism and atheism, our fear of no longer being the strongest and wealthiest nation on earth, and many smaller fears—to justify spending more time, money, and energy to build more devastating weapons, our planet will have little chance of surviving into the next century. We *must* move out of the place of death wishes and death threats and search, as nations, for ways of international reconciliation, cooperation, and care. We indeed need academies of peace, ministries of peace, and peacekeeping forces. We need educational reform, church reform, and even entertainment reform that makes peace its main concern. We need a new economic order beyond socialism and capitalism which makes justice for all its goal. But most of all, we need to believe as nations that a new international order is possible, and that the rivalries between countries or blocs of countries are as outdated as the medieval rivalries between cities. This is what "global ecstasy" is all about. It is the movement from fear to love, from death to life, from stagnation to rebirth, from living as rivals to living as people who belong to one human community.

To speak this way is to dream great dreams. It is like composing a new symphony that, once created, sounds familiar. The Fifth Symphony of Beethoven now sounds as if it always existed. We find it so familiar that we can hardly believe there was once a time without it, and that each movement had to be conceived note by note by a human being. It was not written in the stars, it had to be made. So too, new ways must be found for nations to lift up their unity in global celebration, and praise the Creator in ecstatic, joyful song. Most people despair that such a peace is possible. They cling to old ways and prefer the security offered by preparing for war to the insecurity of taking risks for peace. But the few who dare to sing a new song of peace are the new St. Francises of our time. They offer a glimpse of a new order that is being born out of the ruin of the old. The world is waiting for new saints, ecstatic men and women who are so deeply rooted in the love of God that they are free to envision a new international order—where justice reigns and war is no longer the preferred way to solve conflicts among nations.

Here and there, we catch a glimpse of this vision. When Jean Vanier took two handicapped people into his house twenty years ago, he did something that many considered a waste of time and talent. But for him it became the concrete way from fear to love. He believed that in choosing the broken as his family, he followed the way of Jesus. Impractical, sentimental, naïve? Would it not have been better for him to devote his energy and talent to the burning issues of our time? He himself simply did what he felt called to do, but today, twenty years later, young men and women from all over the world are working together in countless homes to care for handicapped people. L'Arche is certainly not a new international order, nor the end of wars and violence, nor the beginning of a new foreign policy. But it is a light "put on the lamp stand where it shines for everyone in the house" (Matthew 5:16). Jean Vanier does not want the light of l'Arche kept under a basket. He writes:

We do not seek to have nice little warm communities which are cut off from the outside world. L'Arche participates in the struggle for justice; it wants to be in solidarity with the poor and the oppressed all over the world; it wants to struggle for peace. But its way of doing all this is different from the ways of large political and social movements.

Our struggle is essentially a struggle for life. We want to affirm that the life of each human being, each person, is important particularly when that person is very poor, very diminished; we try to make this affirmation not by making speeches but by significant actions. We can't participate in the big political struggles or invest our energies in worldwide activities, because Innocente in Bouaké, Vincent in Québec, Françoise in Haiti, and many, many others ask of us a continual presence with them. At every moment, we need to struggle so that each one can find the security and the human presence alongside him or her which is needed to help him or her want to live and grow.

But at the same time, we must support all these movements which struggle for justice. Sometimes we will only be able to be alongside them in heart and encouragement, but at other times we can occasionally bring an effective presence. Let us pray that each of our communities will be in solidarity with those who suffer, and be a place of hope in a world of divisions and despair (Letters of l'Arche, *September 1985, p. 1*).

L'Arche reminds us that a worldwide movement of care for the poor and the oppressed can engender a new consciousness which transcends the boundaries of sex, religion, race, and nation. Such a consciousness can give birth to a world community, a community to celebrate our shared humanity, to sing a joyful song of praise to the God of love, and to proclaim the ultimate victory of life over death.

Conclusion

This brings us to the end of our reflections about ecstasy as the third quality of life in the house of love. The word "ecstasy" has helped us see how essential joy is in a truly Christian spirituality. Joy is radically different from happiness, for it does not depend upon the "ups" and "downs" of our existence. It is the constant moving away from the static places of death toward the house of God, where the abundant life can be recognized and celebrated.

Ecstasy, like intimacy and fecundity, has a global dimension. Seen in the context of a world on the verge of self-destruction, ecstasy calls for a new international order and invites the nations to view their separate identities not as a cause for war, but as unique contributions to the celebration of a common humanity. Only by claiming the global as well as the personal dimension of the ecstatic life in the house of love do we truly witness to the presence of Christ, who came to make *all* things new.

CONCLUSION

Signs of Life

As I come to the end of this book about signs of life in the house of God, I am constantly reminded that we have not made it fully home yet. Letters from Honduras and Guatemala speak of the increasing danger of regional war in Central America, a letter from Northern Ireland says: "the problems have become much worse," the television shows heavy fighting in Afghanistan, hunger in Africa, poverty in Latin America, and violence in the Middle East. The newspapers are filled with stories about the hijacking of the Italian cruise ship *Achille Lauro,* and the capture of the hijackers by U.S. Navy jets. Articles about the meeting of Presidents Gorbachev and Reagan voice great pessimism with regard to stopping the arms race. Whenever and wherever I listen attentively, I hear voices of fear about the future of the world.

In the smaller circles of family, community, town, and city, things don't look any better. Countless homes suffer from division between parents and uncertainty among children, numerous religious communities have not only lost many of their members, but also much of their vitality, and in many towns people don't dare walk alone on the streets at night. In cities like Boston, New York, Paris, and London even middle-class people, unable to find work, are struggling for money and food. And, of course, the poor continue to suffer everywhere.

Regarding the youth of the 1980s, Jean Vanier writes: "They feel powerless in the face of the enormous powers that rule the world. Twenty years ago young people believed they could do everything, and now they are convinced that it is impossible to do anything" ("Jeunes d'Aujourd'hui: un pressant appel à l'Église," in *Vie Consacrée,* September 1985, p. 283).

It is indeed not hard to see the fear that holds the world in its claws. Homelessness, whether caused by fleeing or clinging, fruitlessness, whether expressed as sterility or anxious productivity, and static living, whether in the form of dull routine or rootlessness—all of this should dispel our doubts about the power of fear.

Yet still . . . this book is not so much about fear as about love, not so much about homelessness, fruitlessness, and static living as about intimacy, fecundity, and ecstasy. I want to lift up these signs of life. This book has been written to offer a home, not later—when the bomb has been dropped, the planet destroyed, and all people killed—but now, as we live our fear-filled lives day by day.

Writing this book at the l'Arche community for handicapped people in France, I have become more convinced than ever that the spiritual life—a life in God's house—is not meant for faraway places and times, but for here and now. Only thus can it hold promise for the future. Every day when I hold the bread and the cup in my hands, I pray: "Dear Father, ready to greet your Son Jesus when he comes again, we offer you this living sacrifice of his body and blood." It is the presence of Jesus among us, real and concrete, that gives us hope. It is eating and drinking here that creates the desire for the heavenly banquet, it is finding a home now that makes us long for the father's house with its many dwelling places.

Who better than severely mentally handicapped people can teach us this liberating truth? They do not read newspapers, watch television, or discuss the possibilities of a future disaster. They do not dwell upon the future. Instead, they say: "Feed me, dress me, touch me, hold me . . . Kiss me, speak to me. It is good to be here together now." Mentally handicapped people proclaim with their whole being that Jesus is truly present among us, and that we already have a home, even though we are still on the journey.

As I write this, I realize once again the deep significance of the image Jean Vanier chose to name his community: the Ark. It means safety in the midst of high waves, protection in the midst of heavy rains, direction in the midst of a roaring storm. It means a love-filled home in the midst of a fear-filled sea.

There is no room for sentimentality here. The handicapped people in the ark are not simple, joyful, peaceful people totally oblivious to their fearful surroundings. They carry the fears and agonies of the world in the depths of their own hearts. Their experiences of rejection, segregation, and isolation have marked them for life. It is impossible to be with them for long without being deeply affected by the immensity of their inner suffering and being reminded of one's own. The ark is a house that rocks and rolls on the waves of our times. Nobody remains without some fear.

But Jesus is in the ark, asleep! He is close to us. Whenever the fear becomes overwhelming and we wake him up anxiously, saying: "Save us, Lord, we are going down," he says: "Why are you so frightened, you people of little faith?" Then he rebukes the winds and sea and makes all calm again (see Matthew 8:23–27). The ark is our home, and Jesus has made it his own. He travels with us and continues to reassure us every time we are driven to panic or tempted to destroy others or ourselves. And as he travels with us, he teaches us how to live in the house of love. It is far from easy to grasp his teaching because we keep looking at the high waves, the heavy winds, and the roaring storm. We keep saying: "Yes, yes . . . but look!" Jesus is a very patient teacher. He never stops telling us where to make our true home, what to look for, and how to live. When we are distracted, we focus upon all the dangers and forget what we have heard. But Jesus says over and over again: "Make your home in me, as I make mine in you. Whoever remains in me, with me in them, bears fruit in plenty . . . I have told you this so that my own joy may be in you, and your joy may be complete" (John 15:4,5,11). Thus, Jesus invites us to an intimate, fruitful, and ecstatic life in his home, which is ours too.

A Final Prayer

I would like to end this book with a prayer. It is a prayer of Etty Hillesum, the Dutch Jewish woman mentioned earlier in this book. She wrote it during the height of the Nazi persecution of the Jews in Holland, during World War II. She expresses the central theme of this book more movingly and beautifully than I will ever be able to.

Dear God, these are anxious times. Tonight for the first time I lay in the dark with burning eyes as scene after scene of human suffering passed before me. I shall promise You one thing, God, just one very small thing: I shall never burden my today with cares about my tomorrow, although that takes some practice. Each day is sufficient unto itself. I shall try to help You, God, to stop my strength ebbing away, though I cannot vouch for it in advance . . . All that really matters is that we safeguard that little piece of You, God, in ourselves. And perhaps in oth-

ers as well. Alas, there doesn't seem to be much You Yourself can do about our circumstances, about our lives. Neither do I hold You responsible . . . but we must . . . defend Your dwelling place inside us to the last. There are, it is true, some who, even at this late stage, are putting their vacuum cleaners and silver forks and spoons in safe keeping instead of guarding You, dear God. And there are those who want to put their bodies in safe keeping but who are nothing more now than a shelter for a thousand fears and bitter feelings. And they say, "I shan't let them get me into their clutches." But they forget that no one is in their clutches who is in Your arms. I am beginning to feel a little more peaceful, God, thanks to this conversation with You. I shall have many more conversations with You. You are sure to go through lean times with me now and then, when my faith weakens a little, but believe me, I shall always labor for You and remain faithful to You and I shall never drive You from my presence . . .

Don't let me waste even one atom of my strength on petty material cares. Let me use and spend every minute and turn this into a fruitful day, one stone more in the foundations on which to build our so uncertain future.

The jasmine behind my house has been completely ruined by the rains and storms of the last few days, its white blossoms are floating about in muddy black pools on the low garage roof. But somewhere inside me the jasmine continues to blossom undisturbed, just as profusely and delicately as *it ever did. And it spreads its scent round the House in which You dwell, oh God. You can see, I look after You, I bring You not only my tears and my forebodings on this stormy, grey Sunday morning, I even bring you scented jasmine. And I shall bring You all the flowers I shall meet on my way, and truly there are many of those. I shall try to make you at home always. Even if I should be locked up in a narrow cell and a cloud should drift past my small barred window, then I shall bring you that cloud, oh God, while there is still the strength in me to do so. I cannot promise You anything for tomorrow, but my intentions are good, You can see.*

And now I shall venture out upon this day. I shall meet a great many people today and evil rumors and threats will again assault me like so many enemy soldiers besieging an inviolable fortress. (From An Interrupted Life, *New York: Pantheon, 1984, pp. 151–52.)*

I fervently hope that Etty's prayer will become more and more my own prayer, and the prayer of all who read this book. Then all of our sufferings and all of our joys will become a song of praise and thanksgiving to God, who has found a home in us.